BBC MUSIC GUIDES

Dvořák Symphonies and Concertos

ROBERT LAYTON

UNIVERSITY OF WASHINGTON PRESS
SEATTLE

Contents

First published 1978 by the British Broadcasting Corporation
Copyright © Robert Layton 1978
University of Washington Press edition first published 1978
Library of Congress Catalog Card Number 77-82650
ISBN 0-295-95505-8
Printed in England

BBC MUSIC GUIDES

DVOŘÁK SYMPHONIES AND CONCERTOS

Introduction

All music, whether it be highly sophisticated or extremely simple, is a response to human experience, a report on our inner life. With some great composers one senses that man's relations with his fellow man form the dominant force in their thinking: in others it can be man's relationship with God, or with the world of nature around him. It goes without saying that most artists reflect all three concerns, but in many one or other tends to dominate. In the Debussy of *La Mer* or the Sibelius of *Tapiola* one feels a preoccupation with nature at the highest level of artistry; that the composer has explored one area of experience to the fullest extent. Both worlds are unpeopled; only the observer and the sea or the forest exist for us. With Mahler, on the other hand, this feeling for nature, though strong, is not in the foreground, except on rare occasions; it recedes in favour of an intense concern for and interest in human relationships and emotions. Tchaikovsky is another case in point; and so, too, is Verdi. With earlier masters, Victoria, Byrd, Palestrina, Schütz and Bach, man's relationship with God overrode all other concerns; and for the different societies in which they lived, religious sentiment was of course a far more vital force in their daily experience. It is so, too, in the symphonies of Bruckner, whose feeling for the grandeur of nature is no less highly developed. In almost all the very greatest artists one finds a harmonious balance of these concerns – men who have an almost Shakespearian capacity to encompass the widest possible range of human experience, to transmute suffering and to heighten one's awareness of life. Present-day urban life, though it has enriched our range of awareness in so many ways, insulates us from many of the discomforts as well as the joys of living closer to the soil. As a result, all too many composers have suffered a spiritual deracination; instead of their music responding to life at first hand, only too often it responds to other *musical* experience, for music is available in a quantity and range totally unprecedented in the history of the art. Thus the pressures of modern society do not, generally speaking, favour the young artist with deep roots in nature, but rather the one who is quickly able to digest and manipulate the most recent additions to the vocabulary of music.

For Dvořák the Czech countryside and its people were the formative influences on his artistic personality. Contact with nature was as vital for him as it was for Delius's muse; and his work radiates a richness and generosity of feeling, tempered by a keen musical discipline, that almost recalls Haydn. Like that master, he inscribed his scores with *Laus Deo* or its equivalent. But if in terms of emotional equilibrium he recalls Haydn, he must be numbered after Schubert and along with his friend and contemporary Tchaikovsky as the most natural melodist of the nineteenth century. The fund of melodic invention on which he could call seems inexhaustible, and its freshness and spontaneity are equally undimmed. Brahms is reported to have sprung to Dvořák's defence, when criticism of his work had been voiced, by saying, 'I should be glad if something occurred to me as a main idea that occurs to Dvořák only by the way'. Although many of the ideas, particularly in the smaller forms, have the naturalness and directness of the folk-inspired *musikant*, others evince a spontaneity that was more apparent than real: as John Clapham has shown,[1] many of the ideas in the symphonies that sound so effortlessly inspired were in fact the product of much revision. Such is the quality of Dvořák's musicianship (and the sophistication of his craftsmanship) that his was the art that effectively concealed art.

Every composer of stature creates his own world. Whether or not the listener can tell what the precise features are that make up his melodic style, his harmonic vocabulary and the way his music moves from key to key, or his characteristic handling of orchestral sonorities, he immediately senses, from perhaps only a bar or two, or even a single chord, the identity of this world. Dvořák is certainly such a master: one instantly identifies the quality of texture, the radiance that illumines scores like the G major Symphony, the *Scherzo capriccioso*, and indeed all his mature music. But Dvořák's musical personality was relatively slow to emerge: the world we recognise as his took some time to shape, and its features are only partly discernible in the early symphonies.

As with all great artists, his early work shows a healthy eclecticism. In his youth he responded with enthusiasm to the bands of wandering musicians that were a familiar feature of Bohemia, and he must have been steeped in the folk-music of his country at a very early age. He learned the violin as a little boy, became a chorister in the church of his native village, Nelahozeves, not far from Prague, and played for the local orchestra, even

[1] Clapham, *Antonín Dvořák: Musician and Craftsman* (London, 1966), p. 341.

6

composing marches and waltzes for it. In 1853, when he was twelve, he was sent to the town of Zlonice to learn German, and was fortunate enough to find an excellent mentor in his headmaster, Antonín Liehmann. From him he learned the piano, the viola and the organ as well as harmony, figured bass and so on; he also played in Liehmann's band. Only a few years later, in the autumn of 1857, the sixteen-year-old boy came to Prague (making the journey in a haycart) to take up his studies in earnest at the organ school, 'no Schubert in composition, no Beethoven as an executant', as Alec Robertson puts it.[1]

It is obvious from his early compositions that Beethoven and Schubert were the composers closest to his heart. Side by side with his studies and his exploration of the classical repertoire, he was succumbing to the spell of Wagner, and by the early 1860s Smetana too had become a focal point of his admiration. Dvořák spent the bulk of the 1860s as an orchestral player, first in a small band conducted by Karel Komzák, and then later in the Czech National Opera orchestra into which the Komzák band was absorbed, and which in the latter half of the decade was conducted by Smetana himself. As a composer Dvořák met with very little success at this time, if by success one means recognition. What these years did witness was a gradual process of self-discovery. Admittedly we know next to nothing of the earliest works: there is an A minor quintet from 1861 with second viola, and an A major string quartet from the following year. But the majority of pieces he wrote during the first half of the 1860s were destroyed, and no doubt the First Symphony would have suffered a similar fate had the score ever returned to his hands.

As it happened, he submitted it for a competition in Germany, but the score was never sent back to him. It found its way into a second-hand dealer's shop, where it was bought by a Dr Rudolph Dvořák (not a relative), and came to light only in 1923, when the latter died. Its appearance, not unnaturally, caused something of a stir, and eventually, in the 1950s, a revised numbering was adopted that took account not only of this early work but of the other posthumously published symphonies. Up to that time only the five published in Dvořák's lifetime were numbered, and their order was determined by date of publication rather than composition. Thus

[1] Robertson, *Dvořák* (*The Master Musicians*, ed. Sir Jack Westrup) (London, 1943, 1964), p. 234.

7

the F major Symphony of 1875 preceded the D major of 1880; but the latter was the first to be published, while the former did not appear in print until 1888, after the D minor of 1874, and so bore the number 3. Šourek's numbering is now common usage, but it might be as well to set down the new and the old numbers, together with the dates of the works, so as to clarify the position:

Symphony No. 1 in C minor	
(*The Bells of Zlonice*)	1865
Symphony No. 2 in B flat major, Op. 4	1865
Symphony No. 3 in E flat major, Op. 10	1873
Symphony No. 4 in D minor, Op. 13	1874
Symphony No. 5 in F major, Op. 76	
(originally Op. 24) *formerly known as No. 3*	1875
Symphony No. 6 in D major, Op. 60	
formerly known as No. 1	1880
Symphony No. 7 in D minor, Op. 70	
formerly known as No. 2	1884–85
Symphony No. 8 in G major, Op. 88	
formerly known as No. 4	1889
Symphony No. 9 in E minor	
(*From the New World*), Op. 95	
formerly known as No. 5	1893

The Early Symphonies of 1865

SYMPHONY NO. I IN C MINOR

Until the end of the 1950s the E flat Symphony (1873) was occasionally heard, but the first four symphonies were uncharted ground for all but a handful of scholars. To all intents and purposes Dvořák's symphonies began with the D major Symphony, the old No. 1, or more accurately the F major, written five years earlier but thought of as No. 3. True, Simrock published the scores of both the E flat and D minor symphonies some years after Dvořák's death, but it was not until the late 1950s that the publication of the others began, both in the form of scores and of recordings. It is no exaggeration to say that they put the last five acknowledged masterpieces into a wholly different perspective and offer the most absorbing study of his struggle for symphonic mastery. First of all, it is transparently obvious from the very opening of *The Bells of Zlonice* that Dvořàk is flexing genuinely symphonic muscle, even if it is far from fully developed or toughened. If one compares the exposition with the corresponding passage in, say, Tchaikovsky's First Symphony (*Winter Daydreams*), with which it is roughly contemporaneous, it is the Dvořák that has the greater sense of symphonic momentum and feeling of purposeful movement; the Tchaikovsky, on the other hand, has the more individual and distinguished musical ideas. It is as if Dvořák deliberately curbed his keen lyrical instinct to serve symphonic ends, while Tchaikovsky's lyrical and imaginative genius was given unfettered rein. In any event, the two works that occupied Dvořák in 1865 showed him responding to the symphonic challenge with enthusiasm and, given the fact that he was still in his early twenties (he was only twenty-three when he wrote *The Bells of Zlonice*), an astonishing degree of success. Of course, the C minor is still a study symphony in many respects: it is clumsily proportioned and the finale is far too long, but the opening shows not only a genuine instinct for symphonic thinking but no mean degree of flair. Even as early as this, the scoring has traces of the luminous quality that is so striking a feature of the mature Dvořák. The trio section of the scherzo is an obvious instance: the musical ideas recall the dance-like tunes that he must have heard with delight from the bands of itinerant musicians who used to call at his father's inn.

The first movement asserts its classical stance right from the outset. C minor is the key, and Dvořák's enthusiasm for Beethoven is not difficult to detect. Šourek[1] and others have noted the similarity in key-scheme between this and Beethoven's C minor Symphony. The work opens with a chorale-like figure on horns and bassoons which, one feels, could well serve as the bass-line of a passacaglia against which bell-like formulas could be superimposed. The main theme itself could hardly be more classical. It is not particularly individual or distinctive in profile, though it is what commentators delight in calling pregnant. It moves stepwise up the melodic minor scale and is in triple time, but it is not until much later in the movement that the full extent of its Beethovenian character emerges: its original stepwise movement becomes triadic and (bars 443 ff.) there are strong overtones of the *Eroica*, or perhaps even more of Schubert's 'Great' C major

[1] Otakar Šourek. *Dvořák's Orchestral Music* (Prague, 1954), p. 351.

Symphony. In a sense, of course, it was to Schubert that Dvořák was closest, not only at this period but throughout his life. The second group, an interesting idea which is also in 3/4 time, has not moved far away in key (it is in the relative major) and is curiously uncharacteristic of Dvořák. (It could almost be by Berwald.)

Ex.1

It is a measure of Dvořák's already considerable expertise that this new idea has subtly been prepared (bars 117 ff., 145 ff.) without in any way impairing the freshness of this tune's impact. A third theme, related to the first, is again in the tonic, C minor, but the exposition as a whole is far from cautious or conventional where key is concerned. Indeed Dvořák modulates quite freely, with a boldness that no doubt he would have disciplined in later years (much in the same way that Sibelius in revising *En Saga* tamed his appetite for modulation and lengthened rather than shortened his pedal points, a fundamentally bolder thing to do). But there are some striking and often dramatic tonal juxtapositions – Ex. 2. Had he ever revised the work, as he did its immediate successor, he would surely have scanned with a cold critical eye the obligatory outbursts of fugue – or rather contrapuntal, pseudo-fugal writing – that crop up both in this movement and in the finale. Imitative part-writing was the recourse of every young nineteenth-century composer anxious to leave his listener in no doubt as to the quality of his academic pedigree and the rectitude of his thinking. However, taken as a whole, the first seems to me the most powerful

Ex.2

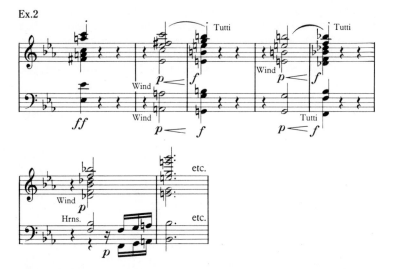

movement in the whole symphony; its sense of purpose never flags; it has fire and a genuine sense of drama.

The slow movement opens with a short four-bar phrase, first in A flat, then repeated in C minor. Its main idea, a highly lyrical one, belongs very much in the tradition of the *Lied*. The tune itself relies for its appeal on the beautiful harmonic sleight-of-hand right at the beginning, which turns the almost Schumannesque idea from the chord of C major very rapidly into F minor. One might suspect that this kind of writing may well have originated at the keyboard, for the accompaniment is confined to harmonic support. Dvořák liked the piano and, according to Suk, his pupil and later son-in-law, he always argued that good music, for whatever medium it was written, should sound well on the piano. At the same time it is worth reminding ourselves that both in his young days and later on, after *Rusalka*, Dvořák did not possess a piano. In this connection, and in spite of Dvořák's later indifference to *The Bells of Zlonice*, one must note that he thought sufficiently well of some of the ideas in this symphony to embody them in his *Silhouettes*, Op. 8, for piano. But if the slow movement has much to commend it, its invention (save for the main song-like idea) is not quite strongly characterised enough to be really good Dvořák. The ending, for example, is far too polite and well behaved to give any impression other than of schoolroom rectitude, and the same must be said of the closing phrases of the trio of the scherzo.

Apart from the first, the scherzo is the finest movement in the symphony. The melodic skeleton of the main idea is basically stepwise, and there is a not-too-distant sense of kinship with the very opening idea. The scherzo of Beethoven's Fifth Symphony is obviously Dvořák's model at the very opening, though there are no motivic resemblances. The trio is unmistakably folk-like and easily the most prophetic passage of the composer to come. Admittedly its second half is discursive, and arguably it upsets the symmetry of the movement. The finale, on the other hand, is undoubtedly the weakest of the four movements. It is enormously long and its invention often falters. Its opening bars are eponymous and clearly suggest *The Bells of Zlonice*, and although the autograph itself does not bear that title Dvořák certainly used it in speaking of his lost symphony. But to be perfectly frank, judged by Dvořák's own high standards the movement lacks concentration and, above all, freshness. The second theme, an oboe figure in E minor, is a really rather lame idea and gives rise to some very laboured writing by way of development, and to our ears becomes dangerously reminiscent both in contour and rhythm of 'Tom, Tom, the piper's son'. The recapitulation and coda are correspondingly prolix, and when the work first came into circulation a version was prepared reducing its length and adapting some of its material.[1] The argument for doing this rests on the valid assumption that had Dvořák had the opportunity he would have submitted the score to rigorous reworking, as he did its immediate successor. It would however be no less logical to argue that he might well have consigned it to the flames, as he did so many of his earlier works. Conjecture is not the wisest counsel in these matters, and it is best to hear this symphony warts and all rather than tactfully refashioned.

---

[1] Since a recording of this version has gained wide circulation, it may well be helpful to enumerate these editorial cuts. In the first movement there are two relatively minor excisions, bars 570–95 and 636–45. In the finale bars 298–323 and 339–402 are cut. At bar 483, bars 12–61 are inserted so as to provide a recognisable beginning of a restatement. The music then resumes at bar 534. Further cuts are 605–35 and 772–803, and there are some slight retouchings to smooth over some of the joins. It should be added that more recent recordings by István Kertesz and Witold Rowicki do not depart from the score as published by Artia.

Dvořák finished work on the First Symphony on 24 March and was already engaged on his Second by the beginning of August. Two months later it was finished, but although it did not disappear as did *The Bells of Zlonice*, it was not performed. Indeed, we owe its immediate survival, in all probability, to the foresight of Dvořák's friend Mořic Anger, a fellow-member of the Opera orchestra with whom he shared rooms. The composer gave the autograph to Anger, who had undertaken to have it bound. However, Dvořák could not afford the sum involved, so Anger, knowing only too well what might happen to the score, held on to it for some years until Dvořák's passion for immolation had subsided. Eventually it was returned to him, and more than twenty years later, in 1887, he made some fairly extensive revisions in preparation for its first performance in March 1888 in Prague, when he was in his late forties, poised to begin work on the G major Symphony.

So what we know as the score has the benefit of the mature composer's critical judgment. As many of the cuts he made survive and are printed as an appendix to the published score, we have a very good idea of what the original was like. He removed about seventy bars from the development of the first movement, about the same amount from the exposition of the finale, and almost twice as much from its restatement. Again, we note that the finale was the weakest movement, predictably enough, and it was on this that his critical eye fixed with appropriate intentness. The bulk of the revision elsewhere affected the harmony, expression marks, texture and instrumentation, while he was also sufficiently enthusiastic to add some ninety bars to the first movement, though he was later persuaded to excise some of them. There is no doubt, however, that in many places (and particularly the slow movement) the Second Symphony represents a considerable step along the road of self-discovery.

Already there is a luminous glow that shines brighter than anything in the First Symphony and that contributes powerfully to the originality of works like the D major and G major symphonies. Much of this glow may be attributable to Dvořák's greater expertise in 1887; but elsewhere, in the slow movement, for example, what one imagines to be the product of revision is more often than not the original. The best single movement by far is this slow movement, even if it is somewhat derivative. Where

Beethoven and Schubert had been the dominant influences in *The Bells of Zlonice* (and indeed continued to cast their shadows much later), here one feels the shades of Schumann that one glimpsed only occasionally in the C minor. Indeed, the song-like opening paragraphs have the distinct feel of the slow movement of Schumann's C major Symphony and emulate its calm serenity. The melodic line soars effortlessly; and although the same charge can be brought against it as its predecessor, the slow movement of No. 1, that it reflects keyboard habits of mind, the charge is weaker and the level of inspiration much higher. True, there is a predisposition towards sequential thinking: between bars 31 and 36 he repeats the same figure no fewer than eight times, a tone lower on each occasion. Later on (bar 61) he lapses into more sequences, but how marvellously scored: widely spaced strings with woodwind comments reminiscent of the magical evocations of nature that distinguish the late symphonic poems. Indeed, this kind of inspired 'woodland' scoring almost recalls *Otello* and *The Wood Dove*, the latter an absurdly underrated masterpiece. One could be forgiven for thinking it an afterthought, since the revision is a good deal closer to the G major Symphony than *The Bells of Zlonice*, but the changes here were relatively trivial – Ex. 3, opposite. The very end of the second movement is strangely poetic if not altogether conclusive, quite the reverse of the close of the scherzo with its Beethovenian overtones: one almost expects the last figure of the first movement of Beethoven's Eighth as an afterthought!

Another passage, fully (or very nearly) characteristic of the mature Dvořák, comes at the very opening of the whole work. Dvořák begins with a glowing chord of B flat into which he weaves some melodic interest: this was in fact an afterthought from 1887, designed, one presumes, to lend density of incident to a texture that was composed of long-sustained chords juxtaposed to striking effect. The B flat is answered by D major, in which the same material is heard and then blazes into a chord of the ninth on the dominant, a really exciting and characteristic effect, particularly with its stirrings of dance-like activity that somehow never surface. It is, one feels, an anticipation of the device in the scherzo where unison strings are answered by woodwind chords, followed by the sounds of a dance coming to life. These stirrings are slightly misleading in that the dance turns out to be a gentle, almost ceremonious melody, rather than something like the wild,

Ex.3

abandoned *furiant* of the Sixth Symphony that the experienced Dvořákian expects.

It must be conceded that the first movement lacks a strongly defined, characterful theme and that there is all too ready a tendency to slip into sequential patterns and square rhythmic formulae. In revising the symphony it was in the two outer movements that Dvořák did not spare his scalpel; the inner movements required much less reworking. As with *The Bells of Zlonice*, the finale is probably the weakest single movement, even if it has good things in it. Among them I would not include the *Tannhäuser*-like second group, and one passage (bars 133 ff.) was of sufficient eloquence for Dvořák to call on it in the opera *Rusalka*. In its original form the symphony must have lasted not much under fifty-five minutes; *The Bells of Zlonice* is a long work too. In his Schubert centenary essay[1] Dvořák argued that 'we should return to the symphonic dimensions approved by Haydn and Mozart. In this respect Schumann is a model, especially his B flat major and D minor symphonies, also in his chamber music. Modern taste calls for music that is concise, condensed and pithy.' It was some years before Dvořák learnt the art of concentration, but even if these first two symphonies are at times derivative and show a certain rhythmic squareness, they both leave the listener in no doubt of their composer's virile symphonic instinct.

Symphony No. 3 in E flat major (1873)

1865 was a productive year. Apart from the two symphonies Dvořák composed a Cello Concerto in A, which he finished in June but never scored, and the song cycle *Cypresses* that followed only a month later. Surprisingly enough, both works survive, but the pattern he had established in the previous two years was soon resumed: once composed, a score was rapidly consigned to the flames. A clarinet quintet was among the many works we know to have suffered this fate; while regretting its disappearance we can only admire the composer's integrity and quietly lament that his example is not more widely followed nowadays. Two quartets from this period do however survive, one in D major and the other in B flat. They do not concern us here, except insofar as the theme of the slow movement of the B flat Quartet turns up in the *Adagio* of the D major Symphony (No. 6) of 1880. This, I think, tends to support Alec Robertson's view[2] that it is exceedingly doubtful whether either Dvořák or Brahms 'destroyed anything valuable to posterity – or indeed whether any composer has ever done so. Any really

---

[1] Published three years before the centenary of Schubert's birth in *The Century Illustrated Monthly Magazine* (New York, 1894), and reproduced by Clapham, *op. cit.*, pp. 301–5.

[2] Robertson, *op. cit.*, p. 21.

good ideas were probably, consciously or otherwise, used up in later compositions.' We find Dvořák using ideas from the early 1865 symphonies in his *Silhouettes*, Op. 8, but this may well have been to ensure the more ready circulation of musical ideas that it then seemed would never gain currency in their orchestral form. It was not until the 1870s that Dvořák started to get performances – and then only of smaller pieces, an *Adagio* from a piano trio, some songs and an early piano quintet.

All this time the struggling young composer was making his living as a violist with the Opera Orchestra, whose fortunes had since 1866 been guided by Smetana. Indeed, Dvořák took part in the first performances of *The Bartered Bride* and *The Brandenburgers in Bohemia*, both in 1866, and *Dalibor* in 1868, occasions that must have stoked the flames of his own operatic ambitions. By this time these were burning fiercely, and his infatuation with Wagner, which had begun as a student, was at its height. He paid frequent visits to the German Theatre in Prague, and according to Clapham 'may well have attended every Wagner performance there'. In any event, his first major works of the new decade were operas, *Alfred* (1870) and the *King and Charcoal Burner* (1871) or *King and Collier* as it is sometimes known, the overture to which Smetana conducted in the following year.

The first two symphonies were composed within a few months of each other. The next two are only slightly further apart and can with good reason be regarded as a pair. Both show the influence of Wagner at its height; both were submitted for the Austrian State prize, which Dvořák won; both were published posthumously a few years before the First World War. With them the tide in Dvořák's affairs began to turn. He started work on the E flat Symphony in April 1873 and it occupied him until the beginning of July. It has been argued that he must have begun the D minor late the same year, for the full score was completely finished in the first three months of 1874. Both works *were* performed in Dvořák's lifetime, so that the common misconception that all four early symphonies were not held in regard by their author is quite erroneous. Dvořák was anxious to see these – and for that matter the B flat Symphony, Op. 4 – in print, and there is enough sheer genius in these works to justify his confidence. Smetana conducted the first performance of the E flat Symphony in Prague in 1874 and included the scherzo of the D minor Symphony, its successor, in a concert only a couple of months later. But a complete performance of the D minor was slow to follow. When his fame had spread and he had established a firm following in England, the Royal Philharmonic Society asked in 1887 or thereabouts for a performance of one of the earlier symphonies, and with this end in view Dvořák embarked on a full-scale revision. But the projected performance never materialised, and in any event Dvořák, who had the great D minor Symphony of 1885 behind him and was an international celebrity by this time, must have been in two minds about the wisdom of presenting an earlier and untried work, whatever its merits, in so exposed a forum. In the end he conducted it himself at a concert in Prague some months before his first American trip in 1892.

The Symphony in E flat has one obvious feature that marks it off from any of the other eight: namely, that it is in three movements instead of the usual four. Whatever else may be said, the whole score leaves one in no doubt as to the strides Dvořák had made in the intervening years in his powers of craftsmanship. The music unfolds far more effortlessly than either of the earlier symphonies and shows a greater organic coherence, even if it falls quite a long way short of the level of mastery of the D major (No. 6).

The opening theme is broader and more expansive than anything in the earlier symphonies. On first hearing, one's thoughts stray (perhaps because of its key) to the Schumann of the *Rhenish* Symphony, but there is little real cause for them to rest there. The contour exudes a Mendelssohnian confidence of spirit and there is even a suggestion of early Wagner; yet the theme could be by no one other than Dvořák, and the harmonies in the bars immediately following the example (Ex. 4) bear his distinct and recognisable imprint.

For all its air of effortlessness and breadth, the theme has two features that mark it out as unmistakably symphonic. First, it has a strong sense of forward movement, a genuinely symphonic flow; secondly, it contains a number of highly characterised segments that can generate further activity. Despite the opening sense of mildness, a second glance reveals the sinew underneath as well as the potential components for the cut and thrust of the symphonic drama. The six semiquavers of the first bar and the upward leap is one component; the others are duly bracketed (*x*) in Ex. 4. Before arriving at the second group, Dvořák launches into what is tantamount to a miniature development of the first, and when we

Ex.4

do get there we discover that it begins with the four descending notes (*x*) in Ex. 4 repeated once *in situ* and then a fourth higher before floating away on a more independent path. Incidentally, these same four notes are to be found in the bass line accompanying the first subject, and according to Šourek the theme derives from this. As if to emphasise this derivation, the roles are, as it were, reversed, the opening phrase of the first subject being pressed into service as an accompanying figure, though it reasserts itself immediately afterwards.

It is no exaggeration to say that this *Allegro* movement is in fact a constant exploration of new facets of its main theme, for very little of its substance does not derive from this in one way or another. Of course, monothematicism as a means of achieving some kind of organic unity was one of the many shots in the armoury of the nineteenth-century symphonist. Schumann's Piano Concerto and D minor Symphony (No. 4) are obvious examples, and composers as widely spaced in time and place as Berwald in the *Sinfonie capricieuse* and Balakirev in his First Symphony had recourse to it. In Haydn, and other eighteenth-century masters for that matter, the same idea could do service as both first and second subject, so laying special emphasis on the tonal conflict that is at the heart of the sonata design. A key chosen on the dominant side of the cycle (in this instance B flat, F, C, etc.) would tend to sound brighter than one on the subdominant side (A flat, D flat, G flat, etc.); and it is in G flat that Dvořák here announces his second subject. In the course of the development it appears in the most distant region of all, A minor, and to much more striking effect.

It is interesting to note that in general, in the mature symphonies in major keys, Dvořák tends to place his second groups in or around brighter key centres. But to tell the truth, whatever the key may be, the theme itself does not belong to Dvořák's most inspired vein. The movement shows more concentration and dramatic flair than we have encountered in either of the 1865 symphonies, though he was not to pursue the experiment of a monothematic sonata movement in any of the later symphonies.

Dvořák does, however, carry his search for motivic cohesion a stage further by echoing in the second movement some of the thematic resonances of the first. The piece has something of the character of a funeral march, the accompanying figure to the opening lament being a reminder of the semiquavers in the first bar of Ex. 4. Another figure from the same theme also crops up on the horns after the first episode, an idea which one could hardly fail to notice, so characteristic is it of the contemplative, nature-loving Dvořák of the later symphonies.

Ex.5

p espress.

The movement is rondo-like in layout, and again a good deal of the material derives from its opening idea. Šourek sees the work as having strong nationalist overtones and argues the possibility of a programmatic basis for the symphony. The first movement, he says, might look back over the historic panorama of the Czech nation recalling 'pride in past glory and grief at past humiliations'. Certainly Dvořák's sense of national awareness had been much coloured by his contact with Smetana, and the success of his cantata *Heirs of the White Mountain*, when it was first performed in 1873, would have given further encouragement to this side of him. There is an element of pageantry in the slow movement too. The feelings evoked seem to lie in the area of public rather than private sentiment: the main theme of the movement seems to lament a public figure, and there seems little sense of personal loss. There are still vestiges of Schumann to be found, but they are much slighter than in the earlier symphonies. Dvořák's absorption in Wagner, Liszt and Berlioz had grown apace in the intervening years, and even the orchestration reflects this. To the classical orchestra of the Second Symphony he adds a tuba, harp and triangle, and the wind section includes a part for cor anglais – though to be fair he had used the latter in *The Bells of Zlonice*. The middle (D flat) section of the slow movement is pure Wagner (the Valhalla motive from *The Ring*) and not a little portentous in effect. But the orchestral layout, though it has not yet the transparency that distinguishes the later symphonies, often betrays its author. Indeed, his scoring in both the E flat and D minor symphonies is a good deal thicker than the mature Dvořák would ideally have approved, though the effect in studying the score, even to an experienced eye, can be misleading, for the scoring often looks thicker than it in fact sounds.

In the finale one feels that Dvořák has, as it were, found himself. The movement is an infectiously high-spirited dance-like rondo. The scoring is brighter and more individual, the texture sparkles, and there is an abundance of vitality and sheer enjoyment of living. The main theme is a delight; but rather than quote it, here is its derivative (the rhythm is identical), with its suggestion of the *Rákóczy March*:

Ex.6

To this is appended one of those counter-themes on the cellos that swirls the dancers along. The movement makes a rather perfunctory gesture at being a sonata-rondo; there is a second subject, in the subdominant, and this recurs in the tonic to open the last statement. It plays no other role in the movement, rightly so since it is not as vivid or characterful a theme as the main idea itself, which derives from the early version of *King and Collier*, occurring in the last act where its rhythm had none of the crisp, sparkling character of its present form.

Symphony No. 4 in D minor (1874)

The D minor Symphony, Op. 13, which followed so soon afterwards, reverts to the usual four movements and has an air of high seriousness as well as a bracing vigour. Its opening sounds a vaguely Brucknerian note, but judging from the bass ostinato figure it is undoubtedly the coda of the first movement of Beethoven's Ninth Symphony which was the springboard for this particular idea and served as an unconscious model. There can be no complaint this time that the two main groups of themes are not strongly defined or adequately contrasted: the first is splendidly virile and has, moreover, no lack of variety. It begins with a rather arresting outburst (Dvořák himself marks it *grandioso*) and is by turn rhetorical (bars 3–6) and dance-like (bar 7 to end of Ex. 7), though the dance is emphatic and stamping, thus generating a tremendous sense of momentum.

Ex.7

Of course the work as we know it was the product of revision in the late 1880s, but the full extent of Dvořák's second thoughts can readily be seen by consulting the notes at the back of the Artia edition of the complete score, which also reproduces the bars that the composer excised from the introduction. This was a wise move, as they hold up the entry of the first subject (Ex. 7) as well as insisting rather unnecessarily on the opening horn motive that plays an important enough role in the movement anyway. As it stands, the movement is well proportioned. The exposition is certainly compact: Dvořák proceeds quickly to the second theme, a tune that has great charm and no little pathos as well. In fact, only the restatement calls for any comment: it is the longest of the three sections, largely because it continues to reassess, as it were, the various characters in the drama.

The first movement of No. 4 is probably the most successfully realised of the sonata movements Dvořák had written so far, and from its success we must assume that he drew the appropriate conclusions: that, temperamentally, his muse flourished within the framework of proven classical discipline rather than in the deeper waters of neo-romanticism. Had his melodic inspiration been of a different kind, the formal plasticity of Liszt and the enormous canvases of Wagner might have been more congenial.

The genesis of the D minor Symphony is not really clear, and it is possible that it was Dvořák's original intention to place the present finale immediately after the first movement. The pagination of the autograph suggests that this may be the case, and we do know for certain that the present scherzo, which started life as a completely independent piece, a *Capriccio* for orchestra, was at one time intended to follow the first movement. However, Dvořák eventually settled on the present and obviously more satisfactory order. It goes without saying that a movement as dynamic as the first calls for a contrast of tempo, and that repose rather than a further irruption of energy is called for. Moreover, both the scherzo and finale are firmly in D minor, and a contrast of key must have been a further consideration in Dvořák's thinking. His slow movement is in B flat major (the subdominant of the relative major), the same tonal area that Dvořák chose to explore for the second group of the first movement, and opens with a long chorale-like theme on clarinets, bassoons, horns and trombones, on which the mantle of *Tannhäuser* hangs very heavily indeed. He delays a cadential resolution of the theme with great skill for seventeen bars, though the bare statement of the fact in flat programme-annotators' prose is pathetically incapable of conveying the beauty of the effect in sound. The movement itself is a set of variations, often very beautiful, but there is no point in pretending that the piece is the equal of his later slow movements.

The scherzo is another eminently spirited movement, with clearly-defined features, vigorous rough-hewn motives and inexhaustible drive. Its trio has an irresistible charm: Šourek speaks of a faint reminiscence of the tailors' motif in the last scene of *Meistersinger*, but it has a strong folk character, both in contour and in its colouring, so that one can more readily imagine the itinerant musicians who so captivated Dvořák in childhood.

Ex.8

The actual shape of the idea is related to one of the main figures in the scherzo itself, a tune to which Dvořák returned later in life, incorporating it in one of the movements of a cycle for piano duet called *From the Bohemian Forest,* Op. 68 (1884).

The finale, like that of the E flat Symphony of the previous year, is not a complex structure; it makes a passing gesture in the direction of sonata-rondo. It, too, maintains the vigour and momentum of the scherzo, and its main weakness lies in the fact that the opening theme, already assertive in character (it is rather like a bad-tempered stamping dance), is insisted upon with perhaps excessive vehemence.

Just as a glance forward to the peaks of No. 6 in D and the great D minor (No. 7) shows how much ground still remained to be covered, looking back at *The Bells of Zlonice* and its companion leaves one in no doubt as to the distance already traversed. Save for the finale, perhaps, the themes of the D minor Symphony have much greater malleability and character. The squareness of phrase structure, a mark of gaucheness in the First Symphony, is far less in evidence; the way in fact that Dvořák handles the *Tannhäuser*-like theme in the slow movement shows how extensive are the strides he had made as a craftsman. He no longer feels the need to pay tribute to the schoolroom, doffing his cap at academic respectability by contriving mechanical fugato passages. The seams in the presentation of ideas are no longer clearly visible, though they have not vanished altogether. Above all his language, though still eclectic, is evolving in both sophistication and independence. It was the encouragement he received with the award of the Austrian State Prize as a result of these two symphonies, and his growing recognition and success, that gave him the impetus he needed to reach out for absolute mastery.

Symphony No. 5 in F (1875)

By the end of the 1870s the tide had turned for Dvořák. Already in 1873 he had left the opera orchestra to earn his daily bread by less onerous means as the organist of St Adalbert's Church, Prague, a post that left him with far more time to compose. He had by now embarked on married life, and his domestic happiness as well as his growing repute unleashed a torrent of creative activity. Alongside the two symphonies of 1873 and 1874 were an octet, three string quartets (Opp. 9, 12 and 16), a violin sonata, a new one-act opera and a full-scale reworking of an old one, *King and Collier*. The following year, 1875, was even more productive: a five-act opera, *Vanda*, the famous Serenade for strings, the relatively little-played but marvellously eloquent Nocturne for strings, the G major String Quintet, Op. 18, a piano trio, a piano quartet, and the F major Symphony. His pen can scarcely have been still for a single moment.

The F major Symphony (No. 5) occupied him for just a little over five weeks, between 15 June and 23 July, and radiates the freshness and warmth of early summer. Although performances of his works were now becoming more frequent (*Vanda* was given four times at the opera in 1876), it was not until 1879 that the new symphony was given its first hearing. By this time Dvořák had received the Austrian State Prize four years in succession and Brahms had taken up the cudgels on his behalf. So far recognition had been confined to Prague: Brahms was anxious to widen these boundaries and secure the dissemination of Dvořák's music on the continent at large. He persuaded his own publisher, Simrock, to take the *Moravian Duets,* and their success began a lifelong association, though not an untroubled one. It was through the championship of Brahms, Hanslick and the Berlin critic Louis Ehlert that Dvořák's music gradually gained ground in Germany and was launched on its conquest of Europe. Joachim played the string sextet, Op. 48, in Berlin and its popularity, together with that of the *Slavonic Dances* that Simrock had commissioned in 1878, preceded Dvořák to England. Ehlert's review of these new pieces in the *Nationalzeitung* is worth quoting:

'I was sitting one day in very bad humour buried in a heap of musical novelties, eye and spirit struggling with the faintness which so easily overcomes us under the impression of empty, indifferent, in short insignificant music, when suddenly two works by a composer so far unknown to me engrossed all my attention: *Slavonic Dances* for four hands and *Moravian Songs,* thirteen duets for soprano and contralto, by Antonín Dvořák. The composer is a Czech, lives in Prague and was, up till a few years ago, a viola player in the Opera there. He has as yet published very few things, but he is said to have a large number of compositions ready, including quartets and symphonies. This is all I could find out about him. To put the matter shortly: Here at last is a hundred per cent talent and, what is more, a completely natural talent. I consider the *Slavonic Dances* to be a work which will make its triumphant way through the world in the same way as Brahms's *Hungarian Dances.* There is no question here of some kind of imitation; his dances are not in the least Brahmsian. Providence flows through this music and that is why it is altogether popular. Not a trace of artificiality or constraint. They could be scored straight away, everything is so effectively and colourfully arranged. To what extent and what material has been taken over into these compositions from Czech folk music I do not know; it is also immaterial. Who asks on seeing Shakespeare's plays on what old Welsh tale, or on hearing Schubert's *Divertissement à l'hongroise* on what Hungarian song, the one or other is based? Here we are confronted with perfected works of art and not perhaps with some pastiche stuck together from scraps of national melody.'

It is not surprising, given this wholehearted advocacy, as well of course as their intrinsic appeal, that the *Slavonic Dances* should have swept across Germany and England taking them by storm, and in so doing making a small fortune for Simrock. The F major Symphony, however, had to bide its time. In fact both the D major and the great D minor (Nos. 6 and 7) were performed and published before the F major made its way outside Prague. When Simrock came to publish it in 1888, he called it No. 3 and changed its opus number from 24 to 76. By this time, some thirteen years or so after its composition, Dvořák's music had fired the admiration of the greatest conductors of the day. Indeed, in accepting the inscribed score von Bülow wrote, 'A dedication from you – next to Brahms the most divinely gifted composer of the present day – is a higher distinction than any Grand Cross from any Prince'. Simrock, of course, knew that a newly-composed Dvořák symphony (or one that appeared to be newly composed) was far more likely to arouse interest and cause appropriate stirrings in the purse than the prospect of something *rechauffé*. Accordingly the String Quartet, Op. 18, became Op. 77, and the glorious *Symphonic Variations* with which Richter scored so signal a success in 1887 moved up from Op. 40 to Op. 78. During the autumn of this year Dvořák took the opportunity of making some revisions of the score prior to publication: most of these were confined to retouching the scoring, and the structural revision, said to have been made before this date, was a cut in the slow movement. This says much for the gigantic stride he took between the D minor Symphony of 1874 and the present work.

What strikes one immediately about this symphony in comparing it with any of its predecessors is the finale. So far the finales of all the earlier symphonies, with the exception of that of No. 3 which combines the function of both finale and scherzo, have been either the weakest or among the weakest of the four movements. The finale of No. 5 is highly original in its handling of key, in its pacing, in its dramatic intensity and function within the structure. Indeed, it is more complex and ambitious than *any* other symphonic movement Dvořák had written up to this point. Šourek goes so far as to place it among his most distinguished movements. One special point is that it sets out in a foreign key, A minor, with which its opening theme is subsequently associated. This dramatic artifice (for this is what it is) is designed to heighten the impact of the tonic key when it does eventually establish itself, and is of course a not uncommon practice among the great classical masters from Beethoven and Schubert onwards. No one, however, made so bold a showing at sustaining this alien key in the face of constant pressure from the tonic as did Dvořák. In fact it takes seventy bars before the combative, concentrated idea that opens the movement and that tenaciously holds off the tonic is eventually transformed into an F major first subject. One passage that stands out in the course of the struggle is Ex. 9 (overleaf), with its magical harmonies and its potent sense of atmosphere. This is obviously an unconscious reminiscence of the famous passage towards the end of the slow movement of the Great C major Symphony of Schubert, where the horns toll bell-like, while the strings undulate between changing

Ex.9

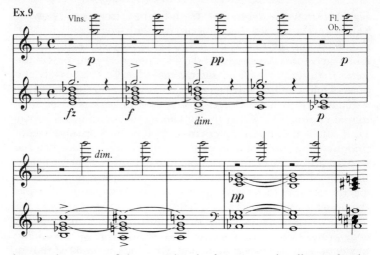

harmonies – one of the most inspired moments in all symphonic literature. The passage must have haunted Dvořák, for one feels its resonances, though in a completely spiritualised form, in the slow movement of the great D minor Symphony (No. 7) ten years later.

Ex.10

Another feature of the movement that is immediately striking is the development, which is both more ambitious and more sophisticated than anything Dvořák had done before. The exposition is relatively short, but the lyrical second theme broadens into some wind chords that shine like some seraphic smile, and that are seen on closer scrutiny to be related to the very opening theme of the whole work. In one sense it seems a pity that this idealised form of the theme does not return at the very end instead of the more literal quotation that Dvořák makes on the brass, arguably the only unimaginative touch in the whole of this inspired movement. These wind chords have brought us to the really distant regions of G flat, a key remote from the tonic F and its would-be usurper, A minor. The development itself is eventful to the point of turbulence: the A minor theme that opened the movement dominates it. The idea is broken down into its various component parts (its second phrase is transformed into a delightful theme on clarinets) as well as returning to assert itself in its pristine form. It once more establishes, briefly, the hegemony of A minor, before the music flows almost imperceptibly back into its proper tonic. Undoubtedly the scale and concentration of the finale establish the symphonic equilibrium that the scherzo, which is as light in weight as a Slavonic Dance, threatened to disturb.

Something else marks this symphony off from its four predecessors: Dvořák's orchestration has now acquired the luminous transparency that we associate with the mature composer. (Of course, some touches *are* mature Dvořák.) The very opening theme, for example, on the clarinets supported by horns, violas and cellos, is beautifully calculated and spaced. The idea itself is among the sunniest, freshest and most captivating that Dvořák ever penned. It could hardly be more pastoral in feeling, but the countryside it evokes is bathed in colouring that is at one and the same time gentle yet vivid. By its side the figure into which it flows is rumbustious to the point of bluster: its repetition (it bubbles away on the wind) reveals another side to its character. It is worth noting that at this point Dvořák's themes acquire an added richness of character and dimension. They can more readily reveal aspects of personality unsuspected on first hearing than be mere melodic shapes that respond to skilful manipulation. Certainly as the movement progresses there is no doubt whatever as to Dvořák's complete mastery of the art of organic thought and symphonic motion. The syncopated figure in the rumbustious F major tune becomes a fresh, expansive transitional idea, and serves to anticipate the rhythm of the second, thus providing an element of cohesion. The second theme is delightfully fresh too – Ex. 11 overleaf.

The movement is compact and masterly. Only in the total overall balance of the four movements does this symphony fall short of the ideal that Dvořák achieved with such consummate artistry in the D major and minor symphonies that were to follow. The slow movement and the scherzo, into which it leads in highly original

Ex.11

fashion, are a good deal lighter in weight than the corresponding movements in Nos. 6 and 7. The slow movement in A minor is *Andante* (it is also marked *con moto*) and has the quality of an intermezzo rather than a slow movement proper. It corresponds in a sense to the kind of idealised dance movement that is to be found in the Tchaikovsky *Polish* Symphony; it concentrates single-mindedly on its charming, serenade-like idea. The middle section, whose theme arises so naturally from the vague melancholy of the main idea (Alec Robertson speaks tellingly of 'its plaintive charm'), is as simple in musical means as it is inspired in artistic effect. Its radiance banishes any hint of melancholy. Whatever their merits, neither of the inner movements is fully commensurate with the inspiration of the first or the dramatic concentration of the last.

Symphony No. 6 in D major (1880)

In September 1879 the third *Slavonic Rhapsody* was given in Berlin, and two months later Dvořák went to Vienna to hear Richter conduct it with the Philharmonic Orchestra there. It was as a result of this success that he had to promise Richter and the orchestra a new symphony. He told his friend Alois Göbl:

I set out last Friday and was present at the performance of my Third Rhapsody, which was very well received, and I had to show myself to the audience. I was sitting beside Brahms at the organ in the orchestra and Richter pulled me out. I *had* to come out. I must tell you that I won the sympathy of the whole orchestra at a stroke and that of all the novelties they tried over, and there were sixty as Richter told me, my Rhapsody was best liked. Richter *actually* embraced me on the spot and was very happy, as he said, to know me and promised that the Rhapsody would be repeated at an extraordinary concert in the Opera House. I promised to come to the performance of the Serenade and had to assure the Philharmonic that I would send them a symphony for the next season. The day after the concert, Richter gave a banquet at his house, in my honour so to speak, to which he invited all the Czech members of the orchestra. It was a grand evening which I shall not easily forget as long as I live.[1]

He did not, however, set to work on the symphony until the summer of 1880, and although much is (quite reasonably) made of its indebtedness to Brahms, whose symphony in the same key had relatively recently appeared, the sketches that he started making show the work beginning life in D minor and also in 2/4. The final sketch was begun in late August and finished about a month later, the scoring then occupying him until mid-October. When he played the work over to Richter on the piano the conductor embraced him after each movement, so enthusiastic was he with the new score. As it so happened, the first performance, which was to have been on 26 December, had to be postponed twice, and eventually Richter, though remaining its dedicatee, did not conduct the première. The Prague Philharmonic had that honour in March 1881 under the baton of Adolf Čech, who had once played the viola alongside Dvořák. and to whom the first performance of the F major Symphony had been entrusted. Richter eventually conducted it in London in the following year, though such was the appetite for Dvořák's music that the symphony had preceded him to the capital.

The D major is one of the very finest post-Beethoven symphonies: its first movement surpasses in breadth and power, and in the naturalness with which ideas are unfolded and grow, almost anything composed between the Great C major Symphony of Schubert and the Second Symphony of Brahms. Although the degree of organic integration in the Brahms symphonies is on a higher level than Dvořák, Schumann, Mendelssohn or Berlioz – I am speaking of the sheer concentration of ideas and their deployment within a musical architecture – this first movement is undoubtedly the first Dvořák worthy to stand alongside Brahms, and in terms of radiance and freshness arguably outstrips him. This is not to say that the symphony *as a whole* is the equal of Brahms's first two symphonies, but it is certainly a masterpiece.

With the D major Symphony one can say that Dvořák's sound world is completely in focus. There are, of course, many expert

[1] Quoted in *Dvořák: Letters and Reminiscences*, ed. Otakar Šourek (Prague, 1954), p. 52.

touches of colour or scoring fully worthy of his art in the earlier symphonies, but heard alongside the *Bells of Zlonice* or the B flat Symphony, Op. 4, the difference is immediately apparent. The thicker textures of their tuttis have given way to scoring that is cleaner and more effectively laid out; Dvořák uses fewer instruments in more telling registers. There are instances of rumbustious scoring after this (the *Carnival* Overture is the most obvious example), but even if Dvořák occasionally overscores, the effect is never muddy as in the early symphonies. Of his orchestration Gerald Abraham has said, 'Generally one feels that Dvořák's music is, if I may invent a word, post-orchestrated – though almost always quite superbly orchestrated.'[1] In other words, there is a distinction between the kind of process that Dvořák's musical thought underwent and the thinking that distinguishes a Berlioz or a Sibelius with whom theme, texture and scoring are only different aspects of the same idea, where the substance and its presentation are indivisible. However, one can argue that there was an increase in the incidence of material conceived exactly in those colours in which it is presented. The cello theme that opens the Eighth Symphony, the flute idea that follows it, the G major theme in the flute's lower register in the second group of the *New World* Symphony, are all instances in point. Elsewhere one can agree that some of Dvořák's scoring is less immediately indivisible, though even in the case of the *Slavonic Dances* there are times when it seems that the sound could take no other form than it does, as with the oboe idea in the seventh dance of the first set. Although there are some Brahmsian tuttis in the D major Symphony, there are passages where the scoring is so beautifully spaced, the texture so open and airy, that one is inclined to think Dvořák one of the most imaginative masters of the orchestra who ever lived.

Brahms's D major Symphony had made its appearance in 1877, and the similarity of mood, key and metre between the two first movements has not escaped critical attention. But although the Brahms is pastoral in feeling the Dvořák reflects a much greater sense of kinship with nature. The Czech scholar Antonín Sychra has argued the close affinity of the original theme that Dvořák planned to use with the Czech folk-song *Já mám kone* – Ex. 12.

[1] G. Abraham, 'Dvořák's Musical Personality', in *Slavonic and Romantic Music* (London, 1968).

Ex.12

Kydž ja jím dám o - bru-ku

This is how Dvořák originally conceived the opening idea, in the minor unlike the folksong, but in 2/4:

Ex.13

It is of course the test of his genius that he should have transformed this idea into the glowing and radiant theme that the definitive score can boast. It is as luminous and innocent as the world of the Nibelungen is dark. The main theme occupies the stage for more than seventy bars, though its course is briefly interrupted by an animated yet disciplined discussion of an ancillary idea before it resumes in full glory. One of the great differences between the apprentice symphonies of 1865 and the mature Dvořák can be found in the quality and character of the invention encountered in subsidiary and transitional themes. The transitional idea here (the figure that begins with four ascending notes, three quavers and a crotchet) is full of character and assumes an important role later on in the movement, giving rise to one of the most imaginative flights of Dvořák's fantasy at the beginning of the development. The second group into which it leads has an enormous generosity of feeling: the first of its ideas is a marvellous cello theme on which a typically Dvořákian counter-subject is superimposed. No one could mistake its identity, while the relaxed lyricism of the cello theme prompts the reflection that Brahms may have been subconsciously swayed by its example in the second group of the first movement of his Fourth Symphony. At the very end the melodic line ascends chromatically, with quite magical effect, into a new and delightfully relaxed idea (Ex. 14 overleaf).

When Dvořák repeats this B major idea in A flat a few bars later the effect is as magical as the means are simple. All in all, the exposition is perhaps the most economical and effortlessly compact that he ever wrote. Indeed, most commentators seem to agree on the unfaltering perfection of Dvořák's inspiration and mastery in this movement. Tovey goes so far as to call the beginning of the

Ex.14

development one of the most imaginative passages Dvořák ever wrote.

No listener can fail to be impressed with its long-sustained chords, from the depths of which fragments of the first theme arise until the basses put them together in a dramatically mysterious sequence. . . . The whole development has all the ease and clearness of Dvořák's methods, with none of the flat reiterations that disfigure his weaker works.

Only one idea remains to be noticed: the emphatic chords that preface the return of the main theme just before the restatement. The whole action is concentrated in the strings; there is a vigorous flourish, after which a step-wise figure of great character marked *pesante* brings us to the chord on the leading-note and after a few bars of tutti back to the first subject and the tonic. (This *pesante* figure recurs with striking effect at the end of the movement.)

The coda must be mentioned. The movement ends with a reference to Ex. 14 in the tonic, D major, and such is the sense of organic cohesion in this movement that one sees it in a new light and feels its kinship of spirit, if not of contour, with the first subject. Certainly its transformation from a tender poetic idea to a sturdy and robust figure is a remarkable one.

The *Allegro* is a movement of genius: the second movement does not quite match the perfection of its proportions or the miraculous cohesion of its thematic substance, though it is all the same a most beautiful piece. Having said this, perhaps one should add that

Tovey, on whom any sensible guide can confidently lean, speaks of it in glowing terms and seems to regard it as in some ways the finest of Dvořák's slow movements.

I know of few pieces that improve more upon acquaintance. It has in perfection an artistic quality which Dvořák elsewhere unfortunately allowed to degenerate into a defect, the quality of a meandering improvisation on a recurring theme, the episodes being of the nature of ruminating digressions rather than contrasts.[1]

Dvořák sets the movement in B flat, and its gentle lyricism and tranquillity of spirit blend harmoniously with the movements that flank it. The opening bars appear to allude to the *Adagio* of Beethoven's Ninth Symphony and have prompted many writers to recall Dvořák's youthful enthusiasm on hearing that work. The resemblance does not stop there: the movements also share the same key and both subsequently move to D major. The movement is virtually monothematic in the sense that its concerns centre on the main idea and material derived from it – a theme that originally came from the String Quartet in B flat of 1862, three years before *The Bells of Zlonice*. The music has great warmth of heart, and it is impossible not to respond to its poetry. Yet whether the theme is rich enough in the range and variety of its resonances to sustain the claims Tovey made on its behalf is another matter. Many will feel, for example, that the first two movements of the great D minor Symphony (No. 7) are more evenly matched in terms of concentration and variety of material, and thus are better balanced in the context of the work as a whole.

With the scherzo, a *furiant*, there is surely no doubt as to its perfection of form, distinction of ideas and superbly characterised material. Its cross-rhythms and its marvellous sense of momentum lend it the kind of exhilaration that only the unleashing of vast reserves of controlled energy can communicate. The trio section explores sunnier aspects of the taut, urgent leading-note-to-tonic figure that opens the whole movement, the textures are open and spacious, and the atmosphere is fresh. The piccolo idea that develops is not only charmingly rustic and poetic but has a poignancy and pathos that are touching. There are no formal ingenuities or innovations here or in the finale. One is reminded of Einstein's words:

Dvořák took over the heritage of absolute music quite naïvely, and filled its forms

---

[1] Tovey, *Essays in Musical Analysis*, Vol. II (London. 1935), p. 91.

with an elemental kind of music of the freshest invention, the liveliest rhythm, the finest sense of sonority – it is the most full-blooded, direct music conceivable, without its becoming vulgar. He drew always from the sources of Slavic folk dance and folksong, much as Brahms had drawn from German; the only difference was that with Dvořák everything was childlike and fresh, whereas with Brahms there was always an overtone of yearning or mystical reverence.[1]

Certainly nothing could be more childlike or fresh than this trio.

It is in the main idea of the finale that one feels the closest proximity to the corresponding moment of the Brahms D major Symphony. Apart from their similarity of character and profile, both have the same sense of forward movement and concentration. Like Brahms, Dvořák also relates his ideas, consciously or unconsciously, with the main theme of the symphony (fig. *x*):

Ex.15

The finale always poses the trickiest problems of balance, proportion and concentration to the symphonist, and many talents have faltered here. Dvořák's own finales, before the F major Symphony, suffered in this respect (all except No. 3 in E flat were overblown), and even in the case of No. 5 some might conceivably argue that the very weight and substance of the finale overbalance the symphony, though this is not my own view. The present finale is a well-proportioned sonata design of genuine breadth whose processes are easy to follow and whose ideas are richly endowed with the variety and vitality without which symphonic argument is impossible. If the Brahmsian mantle hangs heavily over the opening idea, there is no question about the independence, character and mastery of the movement as a whole.

---

[1] Alfred Einstein, *Music in the Romantic Era* (New York, 1947), pp. 301–2.

Symphony No. 7 in D minor (1885)

Five years separate the Sixth and Seventh symphonies. During them Dvořák enjoyed a number of operatic successes: *Dmitri* (1881–2) was staged in Prague; and his earlier opera, *The Peasant a Rogue*, in Hamburg. The first half of the 1880s saw the composition of such orchestral pieces as the *Scherzo capriccioso* and the *Hussite* Overture as well as one of his most concentrated chamber works, the F minor Piano Trio, Op. 65, perhaps his most cogently argued chamber work up to that date. This was also the period of his first visit to London, the first of many, and the beginning of a relationship that was to be both fruitful and enduring. Whatever its failings, the English musical world has always been more readily open to great music from abroad than have its Gallic or Viennese counterparts, and by the time of his first visit in 1884, at the invitation of the Royal Philharmonic Society, Dvořák's music had already made considerable headway. He conducted his D major Symphony, the *Hussite* Overture, the Second *Slavonic Rhapsody* and the *Stabat Mater*. He was much fêted and his reception always enthusiastic.

As soon as I appeared, I received a tempestuous welcome from the audience of 12,000. These ovations increasing, I had to bow my thanks again and again, the orchestra and choir applauding with no less fervour. I am convinced that England offers me a new and certainly happier future, and one which I hope may benefit our entire Czech art. The English are a fine people, enthusiastic about music, and it is well known that they remain loyal to those whose art they have enjoyed. God grant that it may be so with me.

Shortly after this visit the Royal Philharmonic Society elected him a member and asked him to compose a new symphony. Indeed, such a project had been in his mind ever since he had heard Brahms's new symphony (the Third), which had fired his unbounded admiration; and he set to work on it in December 1884, finishing the full score the following March. He himself conducted its first performance at the St James's Hall on 22 April 1885, when the work was immediately acclaimed. Consciously or unconsciously, the symphony may have been designed to dispel the image the English had of him as a nationalist pure and simple. Its depth and seriousness are immediately recognisable, and its stature has never been questioned.

By common consent the D minor has been accepted as Dvořák's

greatest single work, and English critical opinion has accorded it a special status among nineteenth-century symphonies, alongside the Great C major Symphony of Schubert and the four symphonies of Brahms. With the passage of time this judgment, far from being eroded, seems to have gained in strength, for in terms of both inspiration and form this symphony represents Dvořák at his most consistently perfect. The opening idea certainly has a darker colouring and is more pregnant than any other of his symphonies:

Ex.16

It is a commonplace that lyrical ideas rarely make the stuff of symphonic argument, but the genius of this particular idea is that while it has all the potential required for sonata development, including the highly dramatic figure in which it culminates (x), it preserves the sense of songfulness so characteristic of Dvořák at his most natural. It is indeed a bizarre thought that this idea apparently came to him when he was watching the arrival in Prague of the train that brought several hundred anti-Hapsburgian patriots to the National Theatre Festival from Budapest. (Dvořák's enthusiasm for train-spotting is well known, and his knowledge of railway timetables, even during the period when he was staying in the United States, was always prodigiously accurate.) The dark, foreboding element in this idea lightens for a moment when the theme is heard on clarinets in thirds, but the dramatic figure (x) more or less immediately explodes with enormous force, plunging us into the subdominant (G minor). What one hears of D minor in the ensuing paragraphs is a tonic much coloured by this shift. Although it is often pointless to chart a blow-by-blow account of the key changes the musical argument undergoes (any intelligent listener can hear these for himself), this particular tonal colouring is worth mentioning, as it heightens the impact made on the listener by the second subject, which is in B flat, the relative major of G minor. It also happens to be a marvellously sunny, lyrical idea in itself, and is prepared by an exchange of the greatest poetic mastery between wind and strings.

The B flat theme returns in fuller colouring, and with that generosity of feeling that makes Dvořák's textures so distinctive. As Tovey puts it, 'Dvořák, when he is at the height of his power, happens to be a great master of the long meandering sentence that ramifies into countless afterthoughts'. Not that this particular idea rambles; it flows effortlessly, one current taking over before the other has been exhausted. It also mingles with material that springs from the first group (bar 97), and indeed it is the first group, heard in B flat major, that brings the exposition to its climax. The development is one of his most concentrated and shortest: it centres first on the second theme before continuing to explore the seemingly infinite possibilities of the first. Its key contrasts are dramatic and effective; above all they are enormously assured, and a glance at the tonal peregrinations of some of the earlier development sections will show how complete is his mastery. The movement as a whole illustrates the way in which Dvořák, in common with all great symphonic thinkers, does not permit any process in the musical argument to be unrelated to its context; no scrap of an idea is wasted, no figure or melodic detail is thrown up without it having subsequent significance. This is what is meant when one speaks of concentration: certainly the first movement of this symphony is his most concentrated sonata movement of any kind and the one densest in musical incident. The broad framework of the rest of the movement is easily signposted: Dvořák arrives at D minor after having dwelt on the first subject at some length, and so plunges immediately into the transformation to the second. The practice of telescoping the first group goes back as far as the *Symphonie fantastique* and Chopin in the 1830s. In the course of any development, elements of a theme that seem important on first presentation recede into the background, while others whose implications barely register on first hearing spring into prominence. Yet one feature of the great symphonist is his capacity to transform the environment of a theme so that it almost appears to change its character. Certainly the closing bars of the first movement show this imaginative power at its height.

The slow movement is without any shadow of doubt Dvořák's greatest. It begins in B flat, the key of the second group of the first movement, and it is not only the tonality that seems familiar. It is almost as if the second subject has continued quietly developing in the background, transforming itself so much in the process that one can only sense a kinship. The colouring for wind and pizzicato strings further underlines this feeling. The theme bears a superficial resemblance to one of the ideas in the *Hussite* Overture, not unreasonably considering their close proximity. (For that matter, the second subject of the first movement bears a resemblance on paper to the slow movement of the Brahms B flat Piano Concerto, but correspondences of line are not in themselves significant: the idea conveys a wholly different musical experience and springs from a totally different world.) After the wind have stated the theme, the strings enter and swiftly unleash the most natural onflow of inspiration. The next idea is surely one of Dvořák's most poignantly expressive themes, full of the warmth and lyricism that also distinguish him at his happiest.

Ex.17

I have already quoted (Ex. 10) the profound and searching passage into which it flows, with its sighing descending figure and the harmonies that call to mind the tolling of the horns in the slow movement of Schubert's Great C major Symphony. Certainly the relaxed horn solo that follows (in F major) is one of the happiest moments in the whole work. The middle section is darker and more dramatic, and one of the leading thematic protagonists in it derives from the example above. The movement abounds in masterstrokes, not the least ravishing of which is the return of the opening idea on the oboe with a delicate and touching harmonic accompaniment.

It is the scherzo of this symphony that might well have been called the apotheosis of the dance, so captivating are its rhythms and so powerful is its sense of momentum. One may add that its themes are uncommonly distinguished and varied. There is the most effective and exhilarating use of cross-rhythms (3/2 and 6/4), and the music sweeps one along with its abundant spontaneity and vitality.

One would have thought, listening to this movement, that it had composed itself, so natural and infectious is its invention. Yet Dvořák had considerable trouble with the sketch. As is so often the case, spontaneity is purchased at the price of considerable discipline: being spontaneous is not the same as saying the first thing that comes into one's head. The trio shares the perfection of the scherzo, and underneath its bucolic atmosphere there is a carefully controlled nervous energy resonating, as it were, from the scherzo proper.

It is on the finale (*Allegro*) that commentators have focused some criticism: Alec Robertson notes that 'it fails to reach the heights of the preceding ones. This may well be because it lacks the rhythmic variety of the corresponding movement of the D major Symphony and is somewhat square in treatment.' By comparison with the earlier themes, its ideas are more robustly hewn and their phrase structure is more predictable, but by any other standards it need not fear reproach. The themes are bold, their development is vivid, and the movement has all the tragic power and weight that the symphony needs. Nor can it in any sense be said to lack the inspired poetic moments which illumine the best Dvořák. In the final analysis it occupies the same high position in the Dvořákian constellation as its companions.

Symphony No. 8 in G major (1889)

Dvořák's relationship with England may be said to dominate the next few years of his life. Between his first visit in 1884 and the première of the G major Symphony in 1890 he made no fewer than six trips: much of his more substantial output was prompted by invitations and commissions from London and the provinces, and conditioned to a certain extent by prevailing English taste. The oratorio loomed large on the English musical scene, and Dvořák contributed to its repertoire with distinction. *The Spectre's Bride* was written for the Birmingham Festival in the same year as the Seventh Symphony and its first performance was shortly afterwards, on the second of his two visits that year. *St Ludmilla* followed it only a year later, and again Dvořák conducted its first performance at the Leeds Festival. But the period is rich in other fields of creative activity: there is the Piano Quintet in A major, Op. 81, the delightful *Terzetto*, Op. 74, and the underrated Piano Quartet in E flat, Op. 87. It is highly likely that the sense of relaxation and enjoyment these works convey, their freshness of inspiration and their harmony of spirit, spring at least to some extent from the pleasure his new country home was giving him. In the 1880s he was beginning to feel the benefits of his increasing celebrity, and in 1884 he had been sufficiently in funds to buy a small country house at Vysoká. In the ensuing years he spent as much time there as he could.

Not that his financial problems were a thing of the past. There had been shadows over the hitherto friendly relationship he had enjoyed with Simrock. Already at the time of the D minor Symphony, he was setting a more competitive price on his masterpieces and turned down Simrock's offer of 3000 marks for it.

If I let you have it for 3000 marks [he wrote], I shall have lost about 3000 marks because other firms offer me double that amount. I should very much regret it if you were, so to speak, to force me into this position. Although such big works do not at once achieve the material success we could wish, nevertheless the time may come that will make up for it, and please remember that in my *Slavonic Dances* you have found a mine not lightly to be underestimated.

Simrock responded by doubling his original offer but increased his pressure on Dvořák for a further set of Slavonic Dances for the following year. Relations did not improve despite their delivery or excellence, and were further exacerbated by Simrock's churlish refusal to meet Dvořák's wishes that his Christian name should be spelt in the Czech and not the German way. When the score of the G major Symphony appeared, Simrock only offered 1000 marks, complaining that the large works did not sell, and stressed his need for more small-scale pieces. Ignoring Simrock's reminder that he was still bound by the terms of his 1879 contract, Dvořák sold the new symphony to Novello, who had published *St Ludmilla* a few years earlier when Simrock had declined to do so. For a couple of years their relations remained near freezing-point, but after the American trip which put Dvořák's finances on a more secure footing, and the relaxing ambience of Spillville, the breach was sufficiently healed for him to offer the *New World* Symphony, the F major Quartet, and the E flat String Quintet, Op. 97, as well as two smaller pieces, for 7500 marks.

The G major Symphony was mainly written at Vysoká and reflects something of the happiness he enjoyed during the period of its composition. He began sketching it in the summer of 1889 and put the final touches to the scoring in November. Dvořák himself conducted its Prague première in February 1890 and introduced it to London audiences two months later. Richter gave a subsequent performance there and championed it in Vienna, though Dvořák was not present at its first performance in the Austrian capital.

Dear bad Friend,

You would certainly have been pleased with this performance. All of us felt that it is a magnificent work, and so we were all enthusiastic. Brahms dined with me after the performance and we drank to the health of the unfortunately absent father of No. 4. *Vivat sequens!*

Your devoted
Hans Richter

The symphony does mark a new departure in Dvořák's symphonic career. Up to this point his energies had been directed to mastering the art of sonata thinking, without in any way departing from traditional practice. The G major Symphony shows a far greater degree of formal experimentation. Indeed, Dvořák himself left no doubt of his intention to write a work 'different from the other symphonies, with individual thoughts worked out in a new way'. Both the outer movements break new ground as far as he is concerned, and the second movement has much more the character of a pastoral mood-painting than the slow movements of either of the preceding symphonies. Not that the listener is likely to be much concerned about matters of form or structure, so delightful and abundant is the flow of invention. Dvořák could not help writing good tunes, even if he had to struggle to fashion them into their final shape.

Unlike the D minor and D major symphonies, which plunge directly into the action of the drama, the G major is prefaced by a short introduction. This is very different from the 'preparatory' mood Dvořák set in the opening measures of the Symphony No. 4 in D minor: here we have a cello theme of great eloquence and breadth that plays an active though by no means dominating role in the movement. It recurs at the junction of exposition and development, and then again appears in triumph at the beginning

43

of the reprise. It also serves to fertilise the first group itself. This G minor theme unfolds and soon gives way to a first group that is among the most richly stocked and varied in all Dvořák. It begins with an exquisitely innocent flute theme, beginning with a rising G major triad, and answered by a slightly tentative response from the strings. There follows a tremendous surge of activity which reveals the innocent flute idea to be composed of sterner stuff than might have been imagined. Then a second element in the first group takes the stage: it is heard on violas and cellos and grows out of bars 7 and 8 of the introductory theme:

Ex.18

Ideas flow thick and fast, and strengthen the impression that this is the most lyrically well-endowed of any Dvořák first movement.

The second group, on the strings with an odd woodwind comment, has a glowing transparency, though the key does not settle down until the wind take over with yet another idea. Again the sense of momentum, of being swept along by an irresistible tide of first-rate melodic inspiration, is exhilarating. Given the beauty of the first idea in the second group, it seems astonishing that Dvořák should not bring it back in the restatement or even refer to it later on. Only a composer of his prodigality of invention can afford this kind of gesture. A second element on the wind (letter E in the score) is an idea to which he does return.

Dvořák has already created something new in his symphonic art. Instead of moulding his ideas into preconceived roles, each of them comes to life and takes over the course of events. In fact, the whole process seems so natural and effortless that the intervention of the composer scarcely seems necessary. It is almost like a great novel where the large cast of characters evolve and develop, and sometimes disappear from the saga, the author acting as a helpless observer of their personal dramas. The development begins by reverting to the flute idea, but subsequent events tend to concentrate on Ex. 18, which is transformed into the most magical and enchanting episode with a delightful flute counterpoint (letter H). Part of the effect of this heavenly passage (and I make no apology for the adjective) is that of its tonal placing: in F sharp, the key of the leading note, thus heightening the effect of light. Another point to note is that apart from the absence of any reference to the opening of the second group, Dvořák also drastically telescopes the first. He makes no reference to Ex. 18, and it is on the subsidiary element (first introduced at letter E) that he concentrates. This movement more than justifies Dvořák's intention to break new ground, but its triumph lies in that it does so without the slightest sense of self-consciousness.

The slow movement is another highly original piece, as relaxed and luminous as the corresponding movement of No. 7 is intense and searching. Though for all that, there is, as Alec Robertson puts it, 'a touch of pain in the opening harmonies that becomes more pronounced later on'. However, it is the poignancy of one who is experiencing great joy and serenity, but in the knowledge that it cannot always remain and so must be savoured to the full. There is a sense, albeit well controlled, of that awareness of the transience of experience that became so febrile a component of the late-romantic sensibility. Though the movement opens in E flat with an idea that bears some superficial resemblance to a piano piece, *In the Old Castle*, Op. 85 no. 3, it quickly moves into C major. It is, however, a C major crossed by occasional shadows: when the strings reply to the simple flute call (letter A), it is the chord of B flat minor to which they proceed that lends a dark poignancy to their sighs. Its pastoral musings are far from unpeopled: there is nothing of the severe climate one is to encounter in Sibelius's later tone-poems, where nature is all-powerful, indifferent rather than genial, and one feels the presence of strange, primitive forces. Very soon there is a sense of festivity in the air. It is astonishing how simply a great master succeeds in transforming a straightforward descending diatonic scale into a stroke of magic, and over it superimposes an equally diatonic idea, yet one so rich in feeling and generous in spirit. Here is the touchstone of the most profound originality, the ability to conceive a wholly individual effect in language that is common coin but which in Dvořák's hands assumes the glitter and vitality of new currency. The layout of the movement is easy to follow, though there is less density of incident, perhaps, than in the D minor. The skill with which Dvořák fashions practically all his invention from the very opening bars shows how organic are the processes of his musical thinking and how supreme is his level of mastery.

The scherzo is altogether captivating, and sweeps one along no less irresistibly than did the corresponding movements in the D major and D minor symphonies. However, its themes soar with a grace and charm that become a waltz; in contrast to the highly diatonic material of the slow movement Dvořák's line assumes a stronger chromatic flavouring, and haunting and expressive use is made of it. The main idea of the trio is an endearing folk-like melody with an underlying gentle vein of pathos. In fact it has operatic origins and comes from his one-act opera *The Stubborn Lovers* (1874), which was withdrawn after its 1881 Prague production. Dvořák no doubt felt (and rightly) that it was far too good an idea to remain in such limited currency. Perhaps the least perfect part of the movement is its coda, which begins enchantingly but whose good spirits spill over to rumbustiousness.

Dvořák's finale is in the form of a theme and variations, which he prefaces by a trumpet, summoning, as it were, the dancers to their place. Although there is an obvious resemblance between the theme and the first subject (the flute theme) in the first movement, namely the emphatic rising G major triad, this was not the idea as it first came. Indeed, it has been shown how slow this theme was in taking shape. The very first sketch bears virtually no resemblance to the theme as we know it, and even the second (Ex. 19a) is pretty far removed. Dr Clapham discusses this more fully and reproduces a number of the processes through which the theme went before it assumed its present form (Ex. 19b).[1]

The movement as a whole cannot be said to be quite the equal of its companions in organic subtlety or in prodigality of inspiration. Much of its invention is characteristically buoyant and attractive, such as the delightful flute arabesque at letter D or the splendidly earthy C minor episode with its hint of peasant festivities, or the poetic return just before letter N. However, it is not unfair, judging the movement by the standards of its predecessors, to say that it is less richly inventive or varied. There are splendid outbursts of high spirits of the kind to which Dvořák was prone in works like *Carnival*, but these are more rumbustious than infectious. Were it not for the relatively earthbound quality of some of the finale, it could be conceivably argued that the G major was Dvořák's greatest symphony, for its combination of an abundant lyricism with formal originality is something he rarely surpassed.

[1] Clapham, *op. cit.*, p. 33.

Ex.19

Symphony No. 9 in E minor 'From the New World' (1893)

By the end of the 1880s Dvořák's conquest of England was complete, and only his American triumphs lay before him. Honours had been heaped on him at home: the University of Prague gave him an honorary doctorate of philosophy; he was elected to the Czech Academy of Art and Science and also received an Austrian order; and in 1891 he became Professor of Composition at the Prague Conservatoire. That same year he made two further visits to England, one to conduct his Requiem at the Birmingham Festival and the other to receive an honorary doctorate at Cambridge.

47

The first approach Dvořák received from the new world came in the spring of 1891. Mrs Jeanette Thurber, the wife of a wealthy New York businessman, was anxious to secure the services of an international celebrity to head her recently-founded New York National Conservatory, and her choice eventually fell on Dvořák. He declined at first, but Mrs Thurber was a person of formidable energy and persistence: she made her terms highly attractive, offering a two-year contract which would leave the composer four months in the year free but would impose an obligation to conduct ten concerts. The salary, 15,000 dollars, was a considerable temptation; and despite his great reluctance to leave Vysoká and his keen dislike of the prospect of an Atlantic crossing, he eventually agreed. He left for New York in September 1892 and remained there for the next three years, though not all was to his taste in America as far as matters musical were concerned. His vicissitudes in his dealings with Mrs Thurber, who was far from prompt in honouring her financial undertakings, are well enough known, as is his overwhelming nostalgia for the Czech countryside in general and Vysoká in particular. It was on this account that he set such store by his visits during the summer months to Spillville, Iowa, where there was a strong Czech community. His pen was far from idle, and apart from such works as the E minor Symphony and the F major Quartet, Op. 96, known until the war years as the 'Nigger' and now as the 'American', there are such masterpieces as the String Quintet in E flat, Op. 97 and, of course, the Cello Concerto, all dating from the first half of the decade.

The E minor Symphony has puzzled many of Dvořák's admirers and champions. Constant Lambert spoke of it as 'fabricated' and Alec Robertson wrote: 'It is depressing to contemplate this work from the heights of the D minor and D major Symphonies, but such depression is not likely to be widespread.' The *New World* is obviously a work of genius, though not in the same sense as the earlier works. The public at large has a strange and almost unerring instinct in these matters. One can compare the work's standing with that, say, of Grieg's A minor Piano Concerto. This is a work of less depth and formal perfection than many other popular classics, and yet, although its weaknesses are abundantly apparent, it has an indestructible freshness, and an inexhaustible directness that enables it to withstand intensive exposure and emerge unscathed. One could, of course, argue that the very success of the *New World* has served to obscure or at least overshadow Nos. 6, 7 and 8, which are all works of greater substance. True, Nos. 6 and 7 are much less often heard in the concert hall and far less generously represented in the gramophone catalogues.

Perhaps the argument could be taken a stage further: for example, Sibelius may have been wise in suppressing an Eighth Symphony, for had it been less substantial than Nos. 6 and 7 it might have damaged them in public esteem. Had it had great popular appeal, it would have detracted from their impact; had it been weak in inspiration and strength like so many of his smaller pieces, it might well have lessened their standing in the public eye and harmed their prestige. Yet even so, one must concede that it is to the Sibelius of the Second and Fifth Symphonies that the larger musical public has found its way. These are the more readily accessible in that their strength can be recognised instantly. If Dvořák had never composed his Ninth, it is far from certain that the Sixth and Seventh would in fact enjoy greater popularity than they do. Indeed, the contrary is arguable. The most popular classics serve to awaken the interest of the big battalions of music-lovers, and even if their interest is not always sustained, the majority of real music-lovers proceed to the less overtly popular masterpieces. For almost everyone, I suspect, the *New World* Symphony is the point of entry into Dvořák's world, just as Beethoven's Fifth or the 'Emperor' Concerto is the key to his. But just what is it that makes the *New World* popular, and in what way does it fall short of the achievement of the earlier symphonies?

Certainly the melodic invention is more variable in quality than it is in the D minor or G major symphonies. It ranges from marvellously fresh ideas, the equal of any in his earlier work, to themes that bear the stamp of contrivance: the main theme of the finale, though beginning powerfully enough, ends with a relatively ready-made feeble flourish. The main idea of the first movement has none of the natural freshness of the opening of the D major Symphony or its two successors. The working-out of some of the material in the finale is more four-square and routine than in the Seventh.

Hadow called the work 'opportunist', and one can understand something of his feeling. Here was a great composer seizing on the folk-music of a people for whom he had undoubted sympathy but into whose art he could have little real insight. Indeed, as far as the

American Indians were concerned, he saw them very much through the eyes of Longfellow, whose *Song of Hiawatha* he had read in translation in the 1860s. Minnehaha's funeral inspired the *Largo*, and in writing the scherzo Dvořák first had the Indians' Dance in *Hiawatha's Feast* in mind. His knowledge of their music was far from deep; and as far as Negro music was concerned, he placed much reliance on a young negro student, Harry Burleigh, who sang many spirituals to him. The extent of his insight can be seen in the interview he gave to the *New York Herald*[1] where he goes so far as to declare that he found the music of the Negroes and the American Indians very similar. He thought, too, that 'the music of the two races bore a remarkable similarity to the national music of Scotland. In both there is a peculiar scale, caused by the absence of the fourth and seventh or leading note. In both the minor scale has the seventh and invariably a minor seventh, the fourth is included and the sixth omitted.' It is clear that the transcriptions to which he was introduced gave him a very imperfect picture of both folk-cultures and one that was undoubtedly adulterated by Western habits of musical thinking. However, in his introduction he emphasises that he has not actually used any of these Indian melodies. 'I have simply written original themes embodying the peculiarities of Indian music, and using these themes as subjects, have developed them with all the resources of modern rhythms, harmony, counterpoint and orchestral colour.'

No symphony of his met with more immediate success than this, and the ovation he received in New York when it was first performed under Fritz Seidl made him feel like a crowned head acknowledging the plaudits of his subjects. Allowing for the fact that it *is* an incontrovertible masterpiece, in what way were Lambert and Hadow justified in rating it below Symphonies 6–8? Is it the self-conscious use of folk-inspired though not genuine folk material? Dvořák was consciously striving for formal novelty in Symphony No. 8, but there is not a trace of contrivance or any sense of disparity between means and ends. There is, it seems to me, some element of contrivance about the thematic material in the outer movements: the first subject of the opening movement cannot be said to match in spontaneity or freshness the corresponding ideas in Nos. 6–8:

[1] Quoted in Clapham, *op. cit.,* p. 87.

Ex.20

In general there is a certain mechanical quality about the development of the material, particularly in the finale, which certainly operates at a much less subtle level than either the D major or D minor symphony finales. At the same time it must surely be agreed that this is more than offset by the splendours of the two inner movements. The C major tune in the trio section of the scherzo is surely as inspired and radiant as anything in the earlier symphonies.

Ex.21

The slow movement too is by any standards, including Dvořák's own, graced by a melody whose fame and popularity are more than justified. Obviously indebted to the world of the negro spiritual, its achievement and glory is to remain thoroughly Dvořákian at the same time. Its scoring for cor anglais (it was not originally intended for this instrument) is said to have been prompted by young Burleigh's voice. Inspiration runs high and in abundance throughout this movement. Indeed the woodland section (bars 90 onwards) is surely not unworthy of Nos. 6–8, and not even familiarity has dimmed the richness and majesty of the famous chords that frame the *Largo* (Ex. 22 overleaf).

The very opening of the whole work is perhaps more problematic; the quality of the ideas themselves does not match

Ex.22

that of the inspired introduction to the G major Symphony. The opening idea is wanting in breadth, an impression doubtless due in part to its sequential structure. The G minor theme that opened No. 8 is long-breathed and on-flowing; the opening of the E minor is exactly the opposite; one is conscious of its four-bar structure, the second and third bars merely echoing the first phrase at a different pitch. After a horn call, this is echoed on the woodwind and promptly interrupted by a three-note figure on the strings, overtly dramatic – and in the hands of insensitive artists, possibly melodramatic. On the face of it, there is little of the subtle alchemy that distinguishes Dvořák's greatest symphonic thinking; on paper it looks almost perfunctory, even mechanical. Yet in some strange way it works, for these ideas, however simple they may be in their musical structure, succeed in generating a strong atmosphere of nature and a sense of dramatic expectation. Indeed, it is its very directness of utterance that ensures its appeal, and it is at this level of 'effectiveness' that the bulk of the exposition operates. The themes are clear-cut and well-defined, and no one can complain of a lack of freshness about the second group or a want of ingenuity in its presentation. It is approached with a mastery that is fully the equal of his finest writing, showing his great harmonic resource and feeling for colour. The second group falls into two component parts: the first in G minor (though with a flattened seventh), and the second a relaxed, delightful idea in G major; both might be added to those themes in the slow movement and scherzo that have something of the feel of Hiawatha to them.

Occasionally towards the end of the development, perhaps one of Dvořák's least interesting, one is struck by the excessive reliance on sequence, but again one encounters the same phenomenon as we have observed in the introduction. On paper the way in which Dvořák returns to the recapitulation has a slightly mechanical ring to it, and the square rhythmic structure of the main theme does not help matters; yet in performance there is an unmistakable freshness and poetry that only the library pedant would fail to recognise. The restatement includes one of Dvořák's most inspired touches: he recapitulates the second group in the remote key of G sharp minor (bar 316), the second element of the group reappearing in A flat major (374). As a whole the movement has a tremendous dramatic thrust made all the more effective by the clarity with which its ideas are presented. Nowhere is this better exemplified than in the closing pages of the restatement, where Dvořák is faced with making the transition from A flat to E minor. There is a triumphant blaze, and the skies seem to glow with the A major fires that are kindled: the effect is masterly and inspired, and it is from this subdominant major area that he returns us to the tonic.

The slow movement is the most deeply felt of the four. The magnificent harmonic progression that establishes the new key of D flat has already been quoted (Ex. 22) and in a sense the key has already been prepared by the G sharp minor–A flat major centre in which the second group of the first movement was recapitulated. This is the dominant of the new movement's key. Moreover, the inspired melody heard at the outset on the cor anglais seems on reflection to bear a distinct kinship to the second group, albeit one that is too subtle to be easily defined. Although this melody has an eloquence that immediately strikes the listener, the ideas that flow from it are in no way less inspired. First, when the tempo quickens slightly, there is a sinuous idea on flutes and oboes which turns the opening D flat major into C sharp minor and quickly leads into one of the most beautiful ideas in the whole work:

Ex.23

This is an idea that obviously arises quite naturally and organically from the thematic substance that has gone before, and from it, in turn, arises the poetic woodland section that forms the central episode of the *Largo,* at whose climax (bars 96 ff.) Dvořák openly proclaims the kinship the listener has felt between the second subject of the first movement and the main theme of this. He combines them, giving the latter to the trumpets, the former to the strings and horns, adding for good measure the main theme of the first movement on trombones. After this the D flat theme returns and with it the air of tranquillity that had opened the movement.

Dvořák also makes reference to the main theme of the whole work (Ex. 20) in the middle section of the scherzo; and no doubt it could be argued that there is a distant relationship between the secondary theme in the scherzo (bar 68) and one of the pendants of the first group:

Ex.24

The scherzo is a superbly vigorous and lyrical movement; so straightforward is its structure that its contours scarcely need signposting. It is exhilarating and wonderfully fresh, much in the same way as is the opening of the finale. The finale, however, is not without its weaknesses: the pace seems a little forced at times and one is not, as is the case in Symphonies Nos. 7 and 8, swept along, barely aware of the actual mechanics of the music's movement. At the very end Dvořák recalls the themes from the other movements in a way that does strike one as a shade stiff (this is not the case, I think, in the middle section of the *Largo*). No doubt the example of Bruckner, whom incidentally he much admired, may have weighed with him, though the practice was a pretty general one in the nineteenth century.

If in terms of intellectual subtlety and concentration the *New World* is not fully the equal of the D minor Symphony or its immediate successor, it lacks nothing in the directness and vivid quality of its ideas or their integration. Take, for example, the transformation that the D flat major theme undergoes in the finale: from the serene presentation it is accorded by the cor anglais in the

Largo its opening phrases are tossed about (bars 155 ff.) in a most engaging fashion. Nor in terms of sheer melodic inspiration need the marvellous clarinet idea that begins the second group (bar 66) fear comparison with anything in any of the great symphonies Dvořák wrote in the 1880s. After its triumph Dvořák was to turn his back on the symphony and pour his inspiration into the two late string quartets, Opp. 105 and 106, the glorious Cello Concerto, and the remarkably imaginative and much underrated series of symphonic poems that were to occupy him in his later years.

The Concertos

Apart from those by Vivaldi, Haydn, Boccherini and Schumann, there had been very few concertos for the cello, and so it is strangely prophetic that Dvořák's very first attempt in the medium should have been for this instrument, whose repertoire he was later to enrich with the greatest of all its concertos. The early A major Concerto is one of the relatively few scores that escaped destruction during the 1860s and, like the first two symphonies, dates from 1865: indeed, its composition was sandwiched in the few months that separate them. Unlike the Second Symphony, to which he did however return, this early concerto was not only *not* revised, it was never even scored. In fact the short score came to light only in the 1920s and was then edited and put into orchestral form by Günther Raphael. His editing went beyond what could be regarded as legitimate and extended even to interference with the harmonies, which in the second group of the first movement he made far more chromatic. Nor did he shrink from 'reshaping' the melodic line where he thought this appropriate. Clapham speaks of his version of the second subject as 'a travesty of the composer's intentions and style. . . . Raphael said he had reshaped (*Neugestaltung*) the concerto, but it would be more accurate to describe it as reshaped and newly composed'. But in any event the work is clearly unlikely to enter the repertoire even as a curiosity, even were a scholar disposed to put Dvořák's sketch into a performing edition. The ideas appear to be genuinely immature, and the composer's decision to put it on one side and not bother to score it would seem to indicate his recognition of this. There are one or two interesting points to note: Dvořák places a short cadenza at the end of the exposition of the first movement; he completely telescopes the first subject in the reprise; he makes little distinction between tutti and solo passages, and there is very little development of the material. Into the Rondo, which Clapham finds the most satisfactory in form, Dvořák inserts a sizeable portion of the material of the opening tutti, and the middle movement, an *Andante,* does appear to offer writing of a more characterful and naturally lyrical quality. At the same time, it is obviously not proper to draw too many conclusions about a work which has only a sketchy piano accompaniment which the composer would obviously have filled out, modified or perhaps wholly recast had he felt interested enough in the project to have finished it.

PIANO CONCERTO IN G MINOR, OP. 33 (1876)

The Piano Concerto is another matter altogether. Whatever its deficiencies may be, Dvořák did complete it himself, and although its appearances in the concert hall are rare (and are likely to remain so), the work at least bears the *imprimatur* of the mature composer. The concerto is, of course, very much later than the A major Cello Concerto and is of good vintage, dating from the summer of 1876, so that it rubs shoulders with the Symphony No. 5 in F major, the G major String Quintet and the magnificent Quartet in D minor, Op. 34. It was composed with the pianist Karelze Slavkovský in mind, and it was he who gave it for the first time in Prague in the spring of 1878. Much has been made of its pianistic ineffectiveness, but it would, I think, be a mistake to jump to the conclusion that it is solely on this account that its appeal is limited. True, the piano writing *is* ineffective, so much so that the score published in the complete edition includes a reworking of the solo part by Wilém Kurz which is undoubtedly more pianistic, though it has not succeeded in bringing the score into the repertory. Some pianists, František Maxian for example, play his version, while others, Richter and Wührer among them, prefer Dvořák's original: one of the work's most persuasive exponents, Rudolf Firkusný, plays a *mélange* of the two. Dvořák himself had often spoken of his intention to rewrite the piano part, and had the music itself moved on a more sustained level of inspiration it is possible that he would have felt more inclined to do so. The invention does however fall consistently below what he was pouring into his chamber music and symphonies, not to mention such heart-melting works as the *Czech Suite* and the Violin Concerto.

The first movement has an unmistakable sense of purpose and nobility, but its contour is too cautious, its stance too academic, to set in train the flow of abundant invention that usually poured so freely from his pen.

Ex.25

The piano writing is, more often than not, unimaginative, but at times it must be said to border on the incompetent, the left hand lamely duplicating the right without even beginning to utilise the full range of keyboard devices in common currency at this time. This is puzzling since Dvořák was by all accounts a formidable pianist, and in later years his writing for the keyboard, in such works as the Piano Quintet in A, Op. 81, is not only thoroughly idiomatic but distinctly characterful. The piano was not, of course, the natural expressive outlet for him that it was for such masters as Schumann, Liszt and Brahms, and his not inconsiderable body of solo piano music can hardly be said to hold the centre of the stage. Indeed, its position is if anything more peripheral than either Janáček's or Smetana's, both of which occasionally find their way into the recital room or the broadcasting studio. In general it may be added that composers with a very keen awareness of nature, like Berlioz, Wagner, Delius, Mahler and Sibelius, rarely seem to think either fluently or naturally in the monochrome of the keyboard. Debussy is perhaps the only major exception. Dvořák's own lack of feeling for the medium as such may have conditioned the quality of his invention.

The first movement is thoroughly straightforward in shape: an opening tutti lays out the thematic substance though it avoids any presentation of the second group. The solo entry is not effectively judged: it seems likely that Dvořák had the corresponding point in Brahms's D minor Piano Concerto at the back of his mind, since the entry is quiet, almost surreptitious. However, it is not dramatically prepared as in the Brahms, and the keyboard layout, the left hand duplicating the right, is highly ineffective:

Ex.26

The music tends to concentrate attention almost exclusively on Ex. 25, at times seeming to underline a passing similarity with the second group of the first movement of the Mendelssohn Octet. Eventually figure *x* looms into greater prominence and moves us on to the second group, not a strongly contrasted idea and again not well laid out for the instrument:

Ex.27

It then blossoms into a rather Mendelssohnian idea (at letter E in the score), shaped not unlike a chorale, which appears on the strings and to which the piano replies with figuration which sounds like half-remembered echoes of Chopin. Bar 174 almost suggests the descending figures in the latter's C sharp minor Scherzo.

Dvořák's music rarely fails to give pleasure, and the first movement of the concerto is certainly no exception. However, judged by the standards of accomplishment of the F major Symphony of the preceding year, the movement strikes an oddly perfunctory note.

The slow movement, an *Andante*, is ruminative and gentle, and its main idea, though not strongly delineated, is warm-hearted and touching. It is sequential in character and relies on the beautiful sub-mediant inflection on the last beat of the second bar for much of its charm. It is let down by a weak ending that is not made more conclusive by mere repetition:

Ex.28

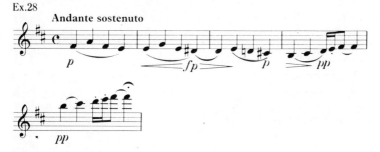

The movement as a whole does not have sufficient variety of substance or mood to be an unqualified success, but it is nonetheless difficult not to respond to its vein of quiet lyricism. The finale, on the other hand, tends to outstay its welcome. It draws for its second group on the G major String Quintet, Op. 77, which is given a vaguely exotic flavouring that suggests the Balkans seen through the eyes of Rimsky-Korsakov, though again this is weakened by a cadential formula that badly hangs fire. The main idea of the movement comes not in the tonic but (of all keys) in F sharp minor. It is lively and dance-like, though again, by comparison with his best ideas, it is shallow and does not really succeed in sustaining interest at its reappearances. The movement is cast in the form of a sonata-rondo.

For all its endearing touches, the G minor Concerto lacks the robustness of invention and generosity of spirit that inform the Violin Concerto of only four years later. The contrast between it and its successor could hardly be more marked: it is as if Dvořák had leapt straight from the world of the Second Symphony, Op. 4, to the Fifth in F major.

Whatever his prowess as an executant on either instrument, Dvořák was much more at ease with the violin than the piano. He had played it as a small boy and possessed that natural feeling for it that seems so widespread in Bohemia and that has produced so many extraordinarily fine string players. One can instance the expert and effortlessly expressive writing in the beautiful Romance in F, Op. 11 (1873), an arrangement of the slow movement of the F minor String Quartet, Op. 9, an outpouring of the most generous feeling, rich in pathos and eloquence. 1873 was also the year of the early E flat Symphony when Dvořák, as we have seen, had just left the Prague Orchestra and was struggling for recognition. By the time the Violin Concerto was begun in September 1879 his star was very much in the ascendant. He had been taken up by Brahms, Hanslick and Ehlert; Joachim had given the Sextet in A in Berlin, and he was poised on the conquest of the German-speaking world and of England. The Violin Concerto is rich in bold ideas, many of folk-inspired origin with strong leaps and sturdy contours, far removed from the pale, academic, cautious stepwise movement that characterises almost all the thematic substance of the Piano Concerto, and which reflect his greater confidence in thinking in terms of the medium. Mention of the folk-inspired nature of the melodic inspiration is a reminder that Dvořák was at this time immersed in the *Slavonic Dances*, the *Czech Suite* and the *Slavonic Rhapsodies*, so that his whole thinking was attuned to its spirit.

The concerto had a relatively chequered period of gestation. Dvořák composed it during the summer of 1879 while he was staying with his friend Alois Göbl at Sychrov castle near Turnov, interrupting its composition by a trip to Berlin at the end of July, when in all probability he discussed the work with Joachim. In any event he sent the score to the great violinist at the end of November, together with a dedication. We have little idea what form the concerto took at this stage, although four pages of sketch for the finale do survive. These bear little relationship with the concerto in its definitive form. After acknowledging the dedication, Joachim later suggested that the work would benefit from thorough-going revision, and Dvořák's oft-quoted letter to Simrock in the summer of 1880 makes it clear that he had acted on Joachim's advice.

I worked most carefully over the whole concerto, without missing a single bar. This will certainly please him. I put the greatest effort into it, and the concerto has been completely transformed. Besides retaining some themes, I added several new ones, but the whole conception of the work is different. The harmonisation, the orchestration, the rhythm and the whole development of the work are new.

Joachim, who had undertaken to play the work, remained inactive for some two years and then, in August 1882, wrote:

I recently took advantage of some free time to revise the violin part of your concerto and to make some of the passages that were too difficult to perform more suitable for the instrument. For even though the whole proves that you know the violin very well, it is clear that from one or two details that you have not played yourself for some time. While working on this revision, I was struck by the many beauties of your work, which it will be a pleasure for me to perform. Speaking with the utmost sincerity, may I say, without the danger of being misunderstood, that I still do not think the Violin Concerto in its present form ready for public presentation, particularly on account of the orchestral part, which is rather heavily scored. I should prefer you to find this out for yourself by playing the work through with me.

Dvořák went to Berlin during the autumn and Joachim played the work at a rehearsal of the Hochschule Orchestra, with the result that the composer made further changes: some figuration in the solo violin part in the first movement and again in the finale was modified, along with some details of scoring. Dvořák also made cuts in the finale, but at the same time strongly resisted the suggestion by one of Simrock's advisers to separate the first two movements, for he felt that the opening *Allegro* would be gravely weakened structurally by so doing.

In the event Joachim did not play the work at its first performance: the honour fell to František Ondříček, who gave it at Prague under Mořic Anger and again in Vienna under Hans Richter in the autumn of 1883. Joachim, oddly enough, never played the concerto in public, though he came near to doing so in London during the period of Dvořák's first London visit. An arch-traditionalist, he was no doubt genuinely unhappy with its irregularities of formal layout, particularly that of the first movement. He is not the only musician to have felt that Dvořák's experiment did not wholly come off.

The movement begins by plunging us directly into the main action: Dvořák omits any kind of introductory tutti. Nor is there a tutti to round off the exposition and lead us into the development. Moreover, the reprise is cut down to a mere thirty-six bars, after which comes a short transition passage linking the movement with the *Adagio*. The movement is undeniably out of balance, but whatever its shape may be, no one can deny that its ideas are of the very highest quality. In vividness and personality they are as far removed from the world of the Piano Concerto as the D major Symphony is from the *Bells of Zlonice*. The opening has the boldness of stride and diversity of character that make it highly effective concerto material. It arrests the attention with a flourish that, while classical in outline, has a strong folk-like flavour, and it unleashes a gloriously Dvořákian melody from the soloist:

Ex.29

This idea is immediately repeated in the subdominant (D minor), whereupon the orchestra seizes on figure *x* and moves towards a poignant subsidiary idea that has distinctly Brahmsian overtones and that blossoms later into a thoroughly characteristic and wonderfully generous idea:

Ex.30

Once again both soloist and orchestra take up Ex. 29, first in the dominant and then in the subdominant, before the soloist returns (at bar 106) with his main theme (Ex. 29, fig. *x*) in A minor and the music moves on, again via Ex. 30, to the second group, a theme of disarming simplicity, directness of utterance and spontaneity of feeling. Although some commentators have noted an indebtedness to Brahms in this particular theme, the folk-like side to its character almost immediately asserts itself when the soloist repeats the theme, decorating it as he does so. After this it never recurs: the development into which the soloist leads us concentrates more or less exclusively on the first group, whose restatement in the tonic brings the movement to an end. In a sense one can well understand Joachim's reaction to what is undoubtedly a lop-sided structure. Clapham complains of the brevity of the second group,[1] and it is so delightful an idea that one regrets its subsequent absence from the score. A still greater weakness seems to me to be the excessive exposure of Ex. 29, which occupies not only the greater part of the exposition but practically the whole of the rest of the movement. Yet the quality of Dvořák's writing is so infectious and songful that structural miscalculations scarcely seem to matter.

The slow movement falls, roughly speaking, into an A–B–A pattern, the first part of which is a long-breathed outpouring of melody. There is a poignant touch towards the end of its course where the harmony is inflected on to the minor chord of the flattened leading-note, thus:

Ex.31

The middle section is in the tonic minor (F minor) and is darker and more turbulent in mood. The soloist's rhetoric seems to have resonances from the first movement, but after it subsides we find ourselves in A flat, where the wind restate the charming main idea. Finally the music, relaxed and ruminative, slowly drifts back into the right key.

The finale positively brims over with first-rate ideas: it is arguably one of the best finales in the whole of Dvořák's output. The main idea has affinities with Czech folk-song and radiates high spirits and love of life. The movement is a sonata-rondo whose landmarks are easily perceived and which teems with a profusion of ideas.

---

[1] Clapham, *op. cit.*

CELLO CONCERTO IN B MINOR, OP. 104 (1895)

More than a decade separates the Violin and Cello Concertos, a period which saw the composition of the remaining symphonies and his successful conquest of England and America. Two smaller works for cello and orchestra precede it, the G minor Rondo, Op. 94, and *Silent Woods*, a transcription of one of the six duets entitled *From the Bohemian Forests*, Op. 68 (1884), one of which is related to the trio of the scherzo of Symphony No. 4 in D minor. In their orchestral form these both date from 1893, two years before the Cello Concerto, the only piece that occupied his thoughts during the last year of his stay in the United States.

When Brahms read the concerto through, he is said to have exclaimed: 'Why on earth didn't I know that one could write a cello concerto like this? Had I known, I would have written one long ago.' Yet apparently no one was more surprised at the decision to write a concerto for the instrument than Dvořák himself. Perhaps the failure of his earlier attempt had discouraged further thought along these lines, and we know that while he much admired the instrument he was far from happy about 'the nasal quality of the high notes and the mumbling of the bass'. Perhaps the two smaller pieces rekindled interest; certainly Victor Herbert's Second Cello Concerto, a performance of which he attended in Brooklyn in 1894, and that composer's cunning in balancing his orchestral forces against the solo instrument may have prompted him to take up the challenge again. Whether because of this or the persuasions of his friend Hanuš Wihan, to whom the work was subsequently dedicated, Dvořák set to work on it in the late autumn of 1894, finishing the complete orchestral score in the following February. Like Joachim, Hanuš Wihan made some suggestions concerning the layout of the solo part, particularly in the first movement, and wanted to add a cadenza in the finale. However, while adopting some of the modifications, Dvořák remained quite adamant about the cadenza, which he refused to countenance under any circumstances.

Again, as had been the case with Joachim, Wihan did not give the first performance of the concerto, although this was not by design but as a result of a series of misunderstandings on the part of Dvořák and the Royal Philharmonic Society. He did play it subsequently, but the honour of the first performance fell to Leo Stern, who gave it under Dvořák's baton during the course of the composer's ninth visit to London in 1896. By then Dvořák had returned to his home country and resumed his professorial duties in Prague. His return to Europe had unleashed a torrent of creative activity. From 1896 come the magnificent series of tone-poems, including such magical works as *The Noonday Witch* and *The Wood-Dove*, as well as two of his chamber masterpieces, the A flat String Quartet, Op. 105, that he had begun in America, and its successor in G, Op. 106.

The Cello Concerto can be said without exaggeration to surpass in mastery any of Dvořák's works composed after the Eighth Symphony. If the Violin Concerto was not wholly successful from a structural point of view, its buoyant high spirits and extraordinary richness and freshness of invention silence almost all one's reservations. The Cello Concerto, on the other hand, has all the virtues of its predecessor together with a mastery of formal design that distinguishes only his greatest compositions like the D minor Symphony. Indeed, the opening exposition has been compared with that of the symphony, and it is worth noting that the sketch of the concerto originally started life in this key. In any event there is no doubt that the two works share the same density of musical incident and concentration of feeling, while the thematic substance of the concerto has all the dramatic potential it requires. Unlike the Violin Concerto, the work opens with a long exposition in which the most pregnant idea at the very outset proves the most commanding and fertile:

Ex.32

The orchestral exposition unfolds in a broad and spacious fashion with this theme holding the centre of the stage. Eventually an ascending figure on cellos and double-basses (bars 37–40) portends the arrival of a second subject and moves the key-centre towards the relative major. There is a risk in presenting the second subject in its contrasting key at this early stage in the movement: the possibility that its subsequent impact in the counter-exposition will be weakened is real. However, the melody itself is so inspired that the risk is slender: Tovey called the idea one of the most beautiful ever composed for the horn, and Dvořák himself confessed that it

meant a great deal to him and that he could not hear it without
emotion.

Ex.33

Its presentation here is finely expansive. When it reappears in the
counter-exposition it assumes greater intimacy and tenderness at
the hands of the soloist. With his entry (not in B minor
incidentally), the material of the movement is re-examined and
new aspects of its personality are explored. The first subject assumes
a dynamic role, and its dominant, masculine features come to the
fore. However, its personality is rich and many-sided, and in the
development section its vein of ruminative, poetic feeling comes
into its own – to what telling effect (see Ex. 34 opposite). During the
development section, which is not long, new light is constantly
thrown on this main idea, and discussion of it is so intensive that
Dvořák telescopes the first group in the restatement.

The second movement begins with a songlike idea, relaxed and
gentle in mood, a perfect foil for the first movement:

Ex.35

This ruminative G major melody proceeds for about forty bars
before a G minor flourish brings us to the middle section. This has
tragic autobiographical overtones. While Dvořák was at work on
the concerto, he received news of the illness of his sister-in-law,
Josefina Kaunitzová, to whom he was devoted. (Indeed, in the

Ex.34

1860s he had been in love with her.) By way of tribute he worked into the *Adagio* the melody of one of his songs, 'Leave me alone', Op. 82, no. 1, which was a particular favourite of hers. She died not long after Dvořák's return home, to the composer's great distress, and prompted by this news he added sixty-odd new bars at the very end of the work, which also refer (though in another form) to the self-same song.

Ex.36

This middle section is music into which he poured great feeling and inspiration before returning to the calmer, more tranquil emotional climate of the opening.

The finale creates an air of expectancy right from the opening bar: the march-like rhythmic pulse has an air of inexorable forward movement. In terms of formal outlay it is a rondo whose fecundity of invention is unusual, even by Dvořák's own standards. He foreshortens its restatement by never referring again to the first episode, leaving the first theme of the second episode to bring us back to the tonic major – the idea is given to the solo violin – before we embark on the lengthy and reflective epilogue. In this the opening of the whole work is recalled, and Dvořák goes on to give vent to his grief at his sister-in-law's death. The concerto was his last major symphonic work, and in no other piece does he give more perfect expression to classical ideals and musical intuition.